Pure Sex, Great Sex

Discovering God's Best for Marriage

BETTE NORDBERG

Pure Sex, Great Sex
Discovering God's Best for Marriage

Copyright © 2013 Bette E Nordberg
All Rights Reserved

Published by Mountain View Publishing
11023 Canyon Road E, Puyallup, WA

All Rights Reserved: No part of this book may be reproduced, stored in a retrival system or transmitted in any form without prior permission in writing from the copyright holder, except as provided by USA copyright law.

Cover and Interior Design: Dallas Drotz, Drotz Design,
   www.drotzdesign.com

ISBN: 978-0-9896411-0-4

Unless otherwise indicated, all Scripture quotations are taken from the Holy Bible, New Living Translation, copyright © 1996, 2004, 2007 by Tyndale House Foundation. Used by permission of Tyndale House Publishers, Inc., Carol Stream, Illinois 60188. All rights reserved.

Printed in the United States of America

For Jeff and Molly,

Your love encourages me.
The adventure you've begun together,
cultivates a lifetime of character and joy
for Eva and Pax.

Contents

Introduction	vii
1 Your Sexuality Matters	1
2 The Power of Commitment	25
3 Clearing the Garden	47
4 The Lies We Believe	71
5 Sex and the Difficult Marriage	99
6 Minimizing Discord Maximizing Sex	117
7 The Rich Harvest	133
8 Considering Inhibitions	159
9 The Body Betrayed	171
10 Going the Distance	195
Wrapup	219

Introduction

Why Purity Matters:

In 2011, the release of one particular fiction title took the publishing world by storm.

What began as a short run book in the United Kingdom quickly became a word-of-mouth phenomenon. Both ABC News and the New York Times dubbed the book, "Mommy Porn," and the controversy surrounding it escalated beyond anything book professionals had previously experienced. By early 2012, electronic sales skyrocketed the title to the NY Times bestseller list. Read on an electronic device, with the cover missing, ordinary housewives enjoyed the book without fear of judgement. When the time came to bring the book to the United States, a frenzied bidding war preceded the contract for a United States publisher.

I became aware of the book more recently, when a cousin challenged me to read it. As an author, I usually respond to such requests by buying the book. I like to know what gets readers excited. In this case, after reading the reviews, I declined my cousin's invitation. With all the books available to me, I chose not to read that particular title. I began to publicize that decision on social media, among my close friends, posting links to other bloggers who had written about their concerns. I was surprised by how many young Christian women had already purchased and read the trilogy.

Why does it matter? Certainly, pornography isn't new. Adult bookstores have long made big money in the United States. Is this kind of fiction really different? Why should anyone care?

Unlike other sexually graphic novels, *50 Shades of Grey* (by author EL James) became mainstream. This book, which features detailed depictions of sadomasochistic sex, had found its way into the hands of very ordinary women. Readers who had never considered this kind of fiction devoured the trilogy in record numbers. The New York Times reported a surge in the sale of rope in New York City hardware stores. Stores which sell sex toys began to feature "Fifty Shades Kits," providing all variety of sadomasochistic toys.

Never before had pornography made such a strong entrance into the mainstream.

And unlike no book before it, 50 Shades has generated controversy even among the most liberal of critics. Doctors, authors, women's rights experts, and even news reporters have expressed concern. Yet, women of all stripes, even conservative Christian women see no harm in reading the books. After all, what happens in my bedroom is my own business, right?

But I ask you, is it true? Does your sexual relationship belong to you alone?

Interestingly, when the issue of human sexuality arises, almost no one seems to care about the one opinion that really matters. *What does God think about your sex life?*

Perhaps you thought God's concern ended at the wedding ceremony. Once you managed to get married, all that "sexual purity" stuff went out the window, right? After all, God only cares about getting you to the altar as a virgin. If you managed that, great. If you didn't, well, that's what forgiveness is for, right? But what about after?

Does He care? Does your sexual relationship with your husband matter to Him? Or does He limit His concern only to those who behave in deviant or frankly sinful ways?

God Cares —Deeply—About Your Sex Life
It matters to Him. In fact, the sexual relationship between a husband and a wife is so intimate, so important, so exclusive, so mutually fulfilling that God has chosen that one relationship as a word picture for His own relationship with his people. In deep and meaningful ways, God's relationship with his people is also exclusive, rewarding and intensely intimate.

But your sex life is not private—at least no more private than any other area of your life. In Psalm 139:7–12, King David makes this declaration:

> I can never get away from your presence!
> If I go up to heaven, you are there;
> If I go down to the grave, you are there.
> If I ride the wings of the morning,
>
> If I dwell by the farthest oceans,
> even there your hand will guide me,
>
> and your strength will support me.
> I could ask the darkness to hide me
>
> and the light around me to become night—
> but even in darkness I cannot hide from you.
>
> To you the night shines as bright as day.
>
> Darkness and light are the same to you.

David understood that even bedroom doors could not separate us from the God who watches over us. While some might view God's all-seeing eyes as invasive or punishing, David's words later in the same Psalm, show us God's oversight as a sign of God's loving care:

> How precious are your thoughts about me, O God
> They are innumerable.

Your loving God is watching.

Time for Reflection

Have you ever found yourself watching or reading something more graphic than you expected? What was it?

How did that experience affect you?

Did that experience change your view of this concept? How?

Does it bother you that God sees everything you do, even in your most private and sexual moments?

Are there things you wish He didn't see?

What to Expect
In the course of this study, you will learn that God cares about your sex life for very specific reasons. He cares because:
- Your married sexual relationship directly reflects his care for and relationship with his people.
- Your sexuality affects every other area of your relationship with Him.
- He made you, and He knows what is best for you.
- Your sexuality is a foundation for the bond you share with your spouse.
- Without sexual purity, the family has no protection.
- Your healthy sexuality is the foundation for the health and strength of your family.

God cares.

Today, more than any time in history, the value of sexual purity is under attack. The evidence is everywhere in American culture: Designers make sexually explicit clothing for elementary-aged children. Modesty is no longer a consideration in fashion. Even wedding dresses are made with see-through fabrics in revealing styles. Today popular magazines tout the arrival of Hollywood's newest infants, many born to happily unwed parents. Extra-marital affairs no longer damage the reputation of politicians or stars. Even family films now depict sex acts in more and more graphic ways. Novels like the 50 Shades trilogy, depicting violent sexuality, are marketed as a way to add excitement to boring sexual relationships.

God Has a Better Way
In the first half of this book, you'll be asked to look at God's biblical

standard for married sexual purity. You'll look for it in stories and proverbs and psalms. You'll look at commands and instructions and consequences. Then, in each section, when you've studied the principles involved, you'll reflect on your own life.

Don't worry. I won't ask you to reveal personal details about your sexual relationship. But you will be asked to think about them.

You can choose to do this study on your own, in the privacy of your own living room. Or, you can study together with a close friend. You might want to get a small group together and tackle this subject with the help of others struggling with the same issues. You could choose to work through the book with your spouse. I've grouped the studies so that you can complete the work in as many sessions as you'd like.

Though I understand that this subject is highly personal, I encourage you to work through this material with at least one other person. Over the years, I have discovered that I process my feelings and thoughts most clearly in the context of discussions and conversation with other believers. It helps me to focus my thoughts, to give words to my fears. If you can, invite someone you trust to work alongside you.

In some of the lessons, I've closed with a simple assignment. Try to do the assignment whether or not you are studying with a group. If you are working with a group, come prepared to discuss what happened and how your work made you feel. You will learn much from your fellow students.

For the sake of understanding, I've chosen to quote all scriptures using the New Living Translation. I won't be arguing technically difficult passages. Instead, in this simple translation, the truth of God's wisdom sings out with simplicity and clarity.

Introduction

This study seeks to accomplish more than simply protect the purity of your sexual relationship. In the last half of the study I will show you ways to cherish and grow your sexual relationship with your spouse. By the time you finish, you will discover that there is much that you can do to build satisfaction and fulfillment—even fun— into the sexual relationship you share.

If you are unsatisfied, this study will show you how you can begin to bring change. If you want to re-think your past choices, now is the time. If you want to build a fence around your own marriage, you will find suggestions here. As you study and reflect on the issue of sexual purity, you can be confident that the God who made you is there to help.

If you struggle with guilt and shame, this study will show you how to experience freedom.

Because after all, He cares.

Time For Reflection
What one thing do you hope to accomplish in the course of this study?

If you could change anything about your sexual relationship with your husband, what would it be?

Pure Sex, Great Sex

Use the space below to turn your hope for this study into a prayer. Simply ask God to accomplish your hopes for you.

A Changing Point of View
Over the last hundred years the moral standards for women have dramatically changed. At the turn of the 20th Century, only immoral women allowed their ankles to show beneath their skirt. A woman needed a chaperone to spend time alone with a man. By the 1920s, specific styles of dancing were immoral. By the 1950s, my mother-in-law's church viewed women who wore make-up as having questionable morals. In the 1960s women's liberation and the sexual revolution brought an entirely new set of values. For the first time, women claimed their right to enjoy their sexuality in whatever context they chose—married or not.

Because God's principles never change (his declaration against premarital sex, for instance), people chose to protect themselves from sin by declaring certain specific behaviors off-limits (spending time alone with a man). By defining additional limits, society hoped to protect young people from progressing into real sin.

Looking back you can see that the line of approved moral behavior became a moving target, changing at the whim of society. For the most part, culture and the church wrote their own definitions of morality, dictating the line of appropriate behavior to young people. Today, our culture has come so far as to reject God's moral standards completely.

That kind of external control can be detrimental in two ways: External controls tend to incite rebellion. After all, no one wants to

Introduction

be told what to do. Rebellion is a natural human reaction to rules and regulations.

External controls also undermine what may be the most important aspect of a living relationship with Jesus Christ. When we rely on what others define as right and wrong, we stop asking God what He thinks of our choices and behaviors. When we stop asking, we stop listening. **When we no longer listen, we may miss out on His specific instructions for our own morality— ones that may actually be more restrictive than that given to the rest of the group.** Let me give you an example:

About 35 years ago, I was in physical therapy school at the University of Washington. My husband was in dental school. His first quarter demanded that he carry 35 quarter hours of classes; most college students carry 15-17. With that kind of schedule, Kim actually chose which subjects to focus on, and which ones he would let slide. When he wasn't in class, he lived in the dental lab, practicing techniques with new instruments on plastic teeth. I rarely saw him, other than when we fell into bed at night. He was endlessly exhausted, entirely focused on dentistry, and not at all on matrimony. It was a hard season in our relationship. I was working hard in school as well, but I missed him.

Then I got a virus. At the time, we'd agreed to care for his young cousins while their parents were away. My throat was so sore that I had it swabbed twice in five days for strep. I stayed home from school, camped out on the couch and slept most of the week.

When I wasn't asleep, I watched the daytime soaps. Since I was half brain dead, I didn't think much about my choice. I didn't see any harm in it. However, one afternoon while lying on our cousin's couch, I remember watching a small television screen framed between my bare feet. I don't remember what show was on at the time, but I was suddenly aware of a very clear instruction. "Turn it off."

I hadn't had much experience with the Holy Spirit in those days. I'd only commited my life to Jesus a couple of years earlier. Though it was not an audible voice, I knew, as surely as I knew my husband's voice, that the Holy Spirit had put a final and permanent end to my daytime soap operas.

At the time, I didn't understand why. Sure, they were cheesy. The writing was bad, and the acting was worse. But that wasn't enough to offend the Holy Spirit, was it? At the time, I didn't ask questions. I simply turned off the TV.

Today, so many years later, I can see the wisdom in His instruction. You see my poor husband didn't stand a chance when compared to these actors. No one wrote his lines, or prompted him to come home with flowers. He didn't have someone to write in perfect behavior—buying the perfect gift, or pouring me a hot bath surrounded by candles. **My husband was human, not an actor who pretended to be a human. I believe the Holy Spirit knew that if I fed that "actor stuff" into my brain, day after day after day, I would only breed dissatisfaction with my own very human, very exhausted, very non-Prince Charming husband.**

Though he is a caring and faithful man, my husband is no orator. Expressing love is difficult for him. He seldom brings gifts, or buys cards. He never writes poetry. Still, I've learned to appreciate all of his effort. Think how differently I might view my husband if, for these past 38 years, I had continually compared him with television's professional husbands. Turning off the television protected me from having Prince Charming of the daytime soaps invade my exclusive relationship with Kim.

Because Jesus knows me intimately, I suspect that this one restriction has saved me from countless moments of dissatisfaction, even outright resentment. It may even have saved my marriage. Only God knows.

Introduction

During this study, we won't be talking much about human rules and regulations. However, I will ask you to think differently about your role in the morality of your church, of your friends, and of your marriage.

Instead of a moral, behavioral line in the sand (drawn by others), I'd like you to view morality in a new way—expecially as it pertains to the body of Christ.

Think of yourself as a circle, nestled in the midst of a collection of circles. Each of these circles represents a person in your church (your local congregation). As with all things, each person is responsible for everything, every decision, every choice occuring in their own small circle.

You choose what you eat. How you exercise. How you pray. How you study the Bible. You choose what you wear. What television or movies you watch. You determine what you will read. All of these choices belong to you alone.

In the midst of your congregation are some who have been injured. Some are weaker. Some struggle violently with sinful habits. Perhaps one man struggles with pornography. One woman struggles with a disappointing marriage. Another is fighting to overcome immorality, or adultery. Perhaps another is deeply lonely and disconnected.

I'd like you to view your own morality—the moral choices you make—as a way to protect these weaker members in your congregation. By surrounding these struggling belivers with strong, morally committed and confident believers, the weakest among us are protected from experiencing the very temptations which threaten them.

Making godly choices protects those who struggle with sin.

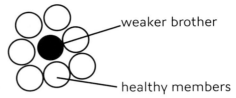

Viewed this way, you can visualize how your moral choices may have vast influence on others in the Body of Christ. What you watch might protect those who struggle with pornography. What you wear might protect a man struggling in his marriage. Your choices are not just your own; they affect the health of your chuch. They still belong only to you; no one can dictate them to you. But for the sake of others, or for the sake of some weakness you may not ever understand, Jesus just might ask you to limit the choices you make.

Keep this in mind as we work through our lessons. I won't tell you what to do; instead, I simply ask you to reflect on how your choices influence others.

And most importantly, I ask you to respond to the quiet, gentle voice of your Shepherd and Counselor. He alone knows all. His requests are never made to restrict your fun. Instead, he wants to protect you and the believers around you, to build you into the most effective, useful person you can become. Obedience, even when you don't understand, brings great fruit. Trust Him.

Time for Reflection

Have you ever experienced a "God moment" where you were asked to restrict your own freedom? What was it? Did you obey? Looking back would you choose the same course of action?

Introduction

In recent years, numerous public personalities from sports, entertainment and politics have admitted to moral failure. Though the details vary, the effect is profound. Both men and women have destroyed their marriages, lost contact with their children, lost professional support and in some cases lost millions of dollars in sponsorship. Thinking back, can you name some of these public personas?

Do you think their morality really mattered? Why?

Can you think of some simple steps these people might have taken to avoid this catastrophic fall?

Up until today, have you considered how you might avoid a similar fall? Or, have you always assumed that you would *never* do anything like that? Are you prepared to consider specific ways you can protect your own sexual purity?

CHAPTER

Your Sexuality Matters

<blockquote>
A nd the more I considered Christianity, the more I found that while it had established a rule and order, the chief aim of that order was to give room for good things to run wild.

G.K. Chesterton, *Orthodoxy*
</blockquote>

Because you hold this book in your hands, I'm going to make some bold assumptions about you, my friend. I'm guessing that you are interested in enjoying the best in married sex. I assume that you care about God's perspective on this sensitive subject. I'm guessing that you have read and believe the Bible to be God's message to His people. And, like me, you probably struggle with the practicality of applying God's Word to your daily life. After all, God has much to say about so many subjects. From finances, to discipline, to church life, God's Word is full of guidance.

Often the message of our culture conflicts with both the message and the intent of God's Word. For instance, you've probably heard someone say, "What happens in the bedroom betweeen two consenting adults is no one's business. God doesn't care about my sexuality." Even believers sometimes warn God away from interfering in their sexuality.

Now don't get me wrong, I'm really good at building a fence around certain struggles in my own life. My language would sometimes shame a sailor. I struggle with my temper, with envy and with accepting truth. Sometimes, I'm ashamed to admit, I tell God, "Don't go there. I can't (or more honestly won't) change anyway, so there's no use talking to me."

In the arena of our sexuality, our culture reinforces our sin nature. We watch helplessly as ordinary television routinely promotes that which God forbids. No matter what terms you use to describe these behaviors—promiscuity, infidelity, sexual affairs, wife swapping, pornography, homosexuality, premarital sex—these subjects saturate our media. Immorality pervades the sketches on Saturday Night Live, the punch lines on prime-time sit coms, and the dramas on television movies.

While believers might recognize evil in its most graphic form, in many ways, we have begun to lose our sensitivity to God's standard of purity. In fact, some believers have even begun to believe that God's standards shouldn't be considered when it comes to making sexual decisions. After all, times have changed!

Since the Bible was written thousands of years ago, it's clearly out of date, out of touch, they say, unreliable for today's needs. After all, "We know so much more today."

Some of us would like to think that God doesn't see what we are up to, that He doesn't care, that somehow, whatever happens in the bedroom between married people doesn't really matter to God. What we really want is a free pass. We think that our God—the designer and creator of the sexual human—should wait patiently outside the bedroom door, while we enjoy complete freedom in an atmosphere devoid of accountability. In this book, I hope to challenge that way of thinking.

You see, God does care. He cares as much about the way you think and express your sexual purity after marriage as He cares about your sexual purity before you exchange wedding vows. He cares both about what you do and what you won't do. He cares about the kindness and love that couples express to one another as they work out their sexual relationship together. In this first chapter, we'll take a few moments to understand why this very personal subject matters so much to God.

As we build this foundation, you might be tempted to feel some dispair about past failures. Please don't give in to those feelings. Remember, this book is not about where you have been; it is about where you want to go, about what you want to achieve. Like me, you may have to deal with past issues. But to build a future, you must choose to leave the past in the past.

Principle Number One
Because God created the male-female relationship, He knows how it works best.

It's true. I don't always rejoice in the spouse God made for me. But thinking about the original married couple, I see God's creative design at its very best. You'll find the story in Genesis, chapter 2:18–25. It begins after Adam has begun tending the garden...

> Then the Lord God said, "It is not good for the man to be alone. I will make a helper who is just right for him." So the Lord God formed from the ground all the wild animals and all the birds of the sky. He brought them to the man to see what he would call them, and the man chose a name for each one. He gave names to all the livestock, all the birds of the sky, and all the wild animals. But still there was no helper just right for him.
>
> So the Lord God caused the man to fall into a deep sleep. While the man slept, the Lord God took out one of the man's ribs and closed up the opening. Then the Lord God made a woman from the rib, and he brought her to the man.
>
> "At last!" the man exclaimed. "This one is bone from my bone, and flesh from my flesh! She will be called 'woman,' because

she was taken from 'man.'" This explains why a man leaves his father and mother and is joined to his wife, and the two are united into one. Now the man and his wife were both naked, but they felt no shame.

In this passage God creates the couple relationship. Take note of the specific details. "It is **not good** for the man to be alone," God says. So, God makes a woman. When he first sees her, Adam's delighted response expresses his longing for someone like himself, someone with whom to share his life. Someone on his own level, who shares his weaknesses, his vulnerability, his "fleshness," his earthiness.

Someone **not** God.

The whole idea of the human couple, of men and women bonding together, of emptiness changing to connection and fulfillment was created by God. In fact the moment is so sacred, so important that the author here interrupts the story to insert a bit of commentary. Moses, the author, wants to make absolutely certain that we understand the moment's divine significance. We read Moses' comment in verse 24.

> This explains why a man leaves his father and mother and is joined to his wife and the two are united into one.
> GENESIS 2:24

Moses tells us that this creation scene, this mutually connected history given by the One God to the two humans demands that the two individuals forever become one—separated only by death.

While Moses might have been referring to the social bond between men and women, the details in the text more clearly convey his meaning—that the man and the woman were naked and not ashamed. Taken in context Moses implies that this oneness expressed in verse 24 refers to their sexual oneness.

Whatever Moses' intent, the passage clearly states that God made the woman both for and from the man. In this supernatural moment, God created something that enabled these two humans to enjoy a special kind of relationship that had, until then, been possible no other way.

Think about the joy and freedom expressed in this story. Imagine being able to stand fully naked in front of someone without experiencing shame. Eve didn't worry about sagging breasts, spreading hips or cottage cheese thighs. Granted, in this moment, Eve must have been created perfectly. Yet standing fully exposed, she felt no shame. (We'll talk more about shame in a later chapter).

Imagine the incredible joy that Adam and Eve experienced in one another as they enjoyed God's great plan. As the designer of this sexual relationship between men and women, wouldn't God know it best? Shouldn't the creator of our sexuality best understand how to protect it, enjoy it, and grow it? Shouldn't He retain authority over it? I think so.

Across from my writing desk, I store a fairly expensive road bike. I keep it there as an encouragement to ride frequently. Each tire bears a mark identifying the maker, the tire size and its ideal air pressure. My tires work best when filled in the range of 80 to 110 PSI. Anything less might lead to pinch flats (where the tube is caught between the tire beading and the wheel rim); anything more might lead to tire failure—a potentially deadly event. The tire manufacturer specifies clear parameters for their safe use.

God, who designed and created sex, cares so much that He too has given us parameters for the safe exercise of our sexuality. He understands how it works. He expresses His care by giving you instructions about the healthiest and most beneficial expression of your sexuality.

The pages of scripture are filled with admonitions about our sexuality. (We'll talk more about those later.) From Genesis in the Old Testament to Revelation in the New, God has made his plan clear. "This," He tells us, "is the only acceptable expression of human sexuality." These restrictions are not simply manifestations of his power and control. Rather, they express His intimate understanding of our human nature, our human weaknesses, and His deep desire that we experience the very best of His design. As Chesterton says, in the safety of these restrictitons we allow good things to run wild.

Time for Reflection

I would love to have been Eve. Can you imagine the joy Adam's greeting must have given her? What emotions and thoughts might lie behind his words?

Think back to your wedding night. What were you feeling? Can you write some of those feelings down?

Where do you think those feelings came from?

These days, when you spend private sexual time with your husband, do you, like Adam think "At LAST!" Be as honest as you can. Write down what you **most often** think and feel.

Principle Number Two
Sexual Expression has Unique Power

Sexual expression can deeply connect two people. It bonds men and women together in spite of life's deepest struggles. From sex we enjoy the exquisite joy of parenting. It brings healing and connection. It's strength rivals superglue!

But when abused, sexual expression can be uniquely destructive.

The human soul has a nearly limitless ability to follow evil. Unfettered, we wallow in selfishness, rebellion, deceit, greed, jealousy, hatred, and unforgiveness. Those sins can be powerfully damaging—moving us away from both God and His people. Still, more than any other sin, sexual sin has a uniquely destructive power. Sexual sin can destroy us from the inside out.

Read the warning below:

> **Run from sexual sin!** No other sin so clearly affects the body as this one does. For sexual immorality is a sin against your own body. Don't you realize that your body is the temple of the Holy Spirit, who lives in you and was given to you by God? You do not belong to yourself, for God bought you with a high price. So you must honor God with your body.
> 1 CORINTHINANS 6:18–21

Did you notice the words "no other sin?" Paul declares here the special and unique power of sexual sin. Because the Spirit of God lives inside of us, our human body contains something precious and holy. Think of the trademarked boxes that the Tiffany Company uses to hold their engagement rings, or the fabled armored briefcase holding the keys to United States nuclear weapons. Neither the box nor the briefcase are to be abused or tossed around. What they contain is too valuable to destroy by deliberate abuse or simple negligence. In the same way, because we carry the Holy

Spirit our precious bodies are not to be used for anything that would in any way mutilate God's Holy Temple.

But sexual sin is unusual in other ways as well. According to the Bible, sexual sin has the unique power to cause both spiritual and/or physical death. While God never fully explains this power, it is clearly illustrated throughout the Word. Read this passage from Proverbs:

> Wisdom will save you from the immoral woman,
> from the seductive words of the promiscuous woman. She has abandoned her husband and ignores the covenant she made before God. Entering her house leads to death; it is the road to the grave. The man who visits her is doomed.
> He will never reach the paths of life.
> **PROVERBS 2:16-19**

Proverbs was written by David's son Solomon. Though he himself is no picture of sexual purity, his passion for truth and wisdom led him to write a book of godly advice. Here, Solomon tells us that the guests of the immoral woman face death. Though never explained, Soloman may refer to different kinds of death.

Is Solomon talking about social death? Has association with the immoral woman caused men to destroy or lose relationship with their wives or families? Have others in the community withdrawn from them because of their foolish decision to frequent this woman? Or is he talking about something more?

Certainly the phrase might refer to physical death. In Solomon's day, little could be done to treat sexually transmitted disease. For centuries, illness has followed infidelity. We know this from both literature and history. While present day lab tests cannot confirm the presence of sexually transmitted disease in ancient history, it is believed that these illnesses may have affected even Roman emperors—where unexplained madness followed lifestyles rife with incest, homosexuality, and multiple sexual partners.

Soloman's advice isn't limited to men. If he were writing to his daughters, the Proverbs passage might look like this:

> Wisdom will save you from the slippery words and expensive gifts of the married man. It will protect you from his false promises and lavish compliments. His promises are empty, though he has made them to others before you. Listening to him will lead you to loneliness, disappointment and death. The woman who listens begins to wither, withdrawing from those who love her. She will be disillusioned. She will end her life alone, spent, used. She will never experience the joys of children, of family, and belonging. Instead, his path leads her to a dark and lonely grave.

But more than social and physical death, sexual immorality has the power to cause spiritual death. Read the following passage carefully:

> I can hardly believe the report about the sexual immorality going on among you—something that even pagans don't do. I am told that a man in your church is living in sin with his stepmother. You are so proud of yourselves, but you should be mourning in sorrow and shame. And you should remove this man from your fellowship. . .
>
> . . .You must call a meeting of the church. I will be present with you in spirit, and so will the power of our Lord Jesus. Then you must throw this man out and hand him over to Satan so that his sinful nature will be destroyed and he himself will be saved on the day the Lord returns. . .
>
> . . .Don't you realize that this sin is like a little yeast that spreads through the whole batch of dough? Get rid of the old "yeast" by removing this wicked person from among you so that you can stay pure.
>
> I CORINTHIANS 5:1–7

Paul is so concerned for the Corinthian church that he instructs them to remove this man from their fellowship. There is no admonition to warn the man, no modern day intervention advised. Instead, this sexual sin is so serious, so grievous, that Paul calls for immediate action. The implication of death is two-fold. Not only is this man's soul at risk (The action is taken to give him an opportunity for salvation.), but the life of the church is at risk as well. Paul explains that the health of the Corinthian church is directly affected by this man's immorality.

That is powerful sin. Do you remember our illustration of circles surrounding one another in your congregation? The idea of protecting one another by leading sexually pure lives comes in part from this very scripture! Sexual sin, according to Paul, has a profound and deadly effect on the people around the sinner. Paul teaches us that sexual sin is so serious a matter that the church should evaluate the health of its members, removing those who consistently and rebelliously fail in this way. Remember, Paul does not speak of those who struggle to overcome sin, but of those who willingly walk in sin. Paul tells us this is our only option to prevent the spread of death among the body.

Time for Reflection

I remember watching devestated, as a friend gave in to sexual temptation. Has someone choosing sexual sin affected you?

Have you ever watched a church discipline someone over sexual sin? Has this study changed the way you feel about it?

Might Paul's concerns about the Corinthian church be valid in today's church? What issues might concern him today?

Principle Number Three
God has chosen the married sexual relationship as a picture of His relationship with His people.

Over the years, I've come to view the Bible as one long story. I see it as a chronicle of God's desperate desire to restore and maintain relationship with his kids. That story began with Adam in the Garden of Eden and continues through Revelation.

In the beginning, God and Adam spent time together. Even after the fall, Adam's removal from the garden, and the continued rebellion of people, God sought relationship. In an effort to start fresh, God repeatedly brings His people to moments where they declare their allegience and dedication to God alone. Examples of these renewal ceremonies are found in Genesis, Exodus, and Deuteronomy. Under godly leadership the people of Israel re-committed themselves to God.

In simple terms, these ceremonies reaffirm the concept, "I am God's and He is mine." In the truest sense, that commitment is similar to the vows of the wedding ceremony, where the bride and groom commit themselves one to another. We can be certain that God takes our commitment to Him seriously. In fact, when His people break relationship with Him, He uses the term adultery. You see the word used frequently when God corrects the idol worship of His people. Here are some examples:

- You have committed adultery on every high mountain. There you have worshiped idols and have been unfaithful to me.
  ISAIAH 57:7
- Look at the shrines on every hilltop. Is there any place you have not been defiled by your adultery with other gods? You sit like a prostitute beside the road waiting for a customer. You sit alone like a nomad in the desert. You have polluted the land with your prostitution and your wickedness.
  JEREMIAH 3:2

- They defiled themselves by their evil deeds, and their love of idols was adultery in the LORD's sight.
  PSALM 106:39
- You took the very jewels and gold and silver ornaments I had given you and made statues of men and worshiped them. This is adultery against me!
  EZEKIEL 16:17

The condition of your married sexual relationship is sacred to God because it represents the committed, mutual blessing of God's relationship wtih his people. When we drag ourselves through multiple sexual relationsips, cloud our sexuality with unhealthy behaviors, use our sexuality to punish, manipulate or control our spouses, when we open our minds and hearts to the world's evil sexual variations, we destroy the very picture God designed to show His loving commitment to the world.

When it comes to reflecting God's perfect love for people, I have to admit that my marriage is a poor likeness. Frankly, I fail in so many ways. It's a good thing that my weakness doesn't tarnish his intent.

God cares that we represent the best of what He has in mind. The married sexual relationship, in its finest form, is the purest picture of God's relationship with His people.

Time for Reflection

I'll confess; I've faced sexual temptation. At the time it happened, I was struggling with depression and my marriage was in deep trouble. I ran into a family friend who sensed my vulnerability. Going in for the kill, he suggested we get together privately, so that he could offer his support during this "difficult time." Though I didn't know it, he was a man who regularly used women under the guise of "support." I admit, outside of friends and God's sustaining grace, I might have succumbed. Think carefully about the following questions:

Have you experienced temptation?

What happened?

What did you do to resist?

Did you tell anyone?

Did anyone help you?

When it happened, how might your friends have given you the most support?

Your Disaster Avoidance Plan
Today every major city has a disaster preparedness plan, ready to activate in response to natural or terrorist disaster. You should have one too, though in your case, it will be a plan to avoid marital disaster.

In the course of these lessons, I hope to give you both the skills and a plan that will protect you from those who would steal your sexual purity and destroy your marriage. In the meantime, if you (like me) are feeling vulnerable in some situation, begin now to do battle. Tell a trustworthy believing friend. Ask for accountability. If you feel you need professional support, seek counseling. The best time to stop an affair is **before** it begins.

Principle Number Four
God expects us to strive for His standard of holiness in every area of our lives.

I can almost hear you groan. "Oh no. Not holiness. Anything but holiness!" I get your point. Even the word is a little old fashioned, isn't it? Still, holiness may be worth thinking about.

If there is any common failure in the modern church it may be this: In our day, we're far too quick to overlook our own failure. We revel in the promise of forgiveness, so much so that we ignore the Bible's clear and repeated exhortation to live holy and pure lives. Having spent many years in ministry, I can't tell you how many times I have watched God's people choose sexual sin over pain, loneliness or longing.

While I depend on forgiveness for my very life, I worry about those who plan ahead for forgiveness while at the same moment making plans to engage in sexual (or any other) sin. I've heard it from wives having affairs, wives beginning same sex relationships, and from lonely wives longing for emotional intimacy with men other than their husbands. **The temptations are strong;** I truly understand. **But there is more at play than our pain.**

The Issue of Holiness.
Christians would never debate the fact of God's holiness. But few believers really understand the magnitude of His purity. Whether we understand or not, throughout scripture God clearly commands that we follow His holy footsteps.

We serve a holy God who expects holiness of His people—a goal that no man or woman can possibly achieve. God understands our sin nature. For that reason he sent His only Son to pay the price for our repeated violation of His holy standards. That price was paid not in coin, or even in gold bouillon, but in blood.

Holy Jesus died so that you and I could assume His (Jesus') holiness before this perfect God. This is not where the story ends. Having assumed, by faith, this gift of holiness, God asks us to begin to exhibit it, to live it out in our lives. **He did not give us forgiveness so that we could go on living as unbelievers. Rather He gave us both forgiveness and infused us with supernatural power, the power to live "other" lives, lives victorious over sin and death.**

Perhaps the best explanation of this principle is found in Romans 6:15–18. Let me share a few verses with you here:

> Well then, since God's grace has set us free from the law, does that mean we can go on sinning? Of course not! Don't you realize that you become the slave of whatever you choose to obey? You can be a slave to sin, which leads to death, or you can choose to obey God, which leads to righteous living. Thank God! Once you were slaves of sin, but now you wholeheartedly obey this teaching we have given you. Now you are free from your slavery to sin, and you have become slaves to righteous living.

When God's expectations are written out, they have a powerful impact over our long held ideas and excuses. As you read these scriptures, let the words sink in. Ponder them. Come back later and read them again. Take note of the emotions you feel:

> When Abram was ninety-nine years old, the Lord appeared to him and said, "I am El-Shaddai—'God Almighty.' Serve me faithfully and live a blameless life."
> GENESIS 17:1

> "And you will be my kingdom of priests, my holy nation. This is the message you must give to the people of Israel."
> EXODUS 19:6

> "Give the following instructions to the entire community of Israel. You must be holy because I, the Lord your God, am holy."
> LEVITICUS 19:2

> For God saved us and called us to live a holy life. He did this, not because we deserved it, but because that was his plan. . .
>
> 2 TIMOTHY 1:9

> But now you must be holy in everything you do, just as God who chose you is holy.
>
> PETER 1:15

> For you remember what we taught you by the authority of the Lord Jesus. God's will is for you to be holy, so stay away from all sexual sin. Then each of you will control his own body and live in holiness and honor—God has called us to live holy lives. . .
>
> I THESSALONIANS 4:2-7

In next week's lesson, I'll give you a chance to think about how you can begin to strive toward His holiness. Like so many goals, this one can seem overwhelming, insurmountable, unattainable. However, the truth is that you can begin to move toward holiness by repeatedly taking small steps in that direction. It won't be easy, but *it is possible*. Just the decision—to pursue sexual holiness—will create ripples in many other areas of your life. You will see change—perhaps even change you don't expect—I promise.

Time for Reflection

If you are human, and you care about the Word, you are probably feeling pretty uncomfortable right about now. As a human, you aren't perfectly holy. As a Jesus follower, you know you should be. For me, that creates tension that is hard to live with. Are you feeling the tension between your holy calling and your human failure? Describe it.

Is there ONE area that gives you the greatest difficulty? (For me, I realize that my language grieves the Father.) Write yours here.

Let me help you begin your journey toward holiness. Tell God that you are aware of His holy standards for your life. Agree with Him that those standards are right and good. Tell Him in your own words, just as you would tell a friend, about your area of struggle. Ask Him to show you one thing you might do today that might bring you freedom from this struggle. Then pause and wait. See if you don't hear the Holy Spirit give you divine direction. Write that direction here.

Working toward Holiness
If you are like me, you might be feeling a little overwhelmed at God's expectations for you. In spite of my best intentions to clean up my act, I usually mess up before I finish breakfast. Though you might make it through lunch, I'll bet you sometimes get discouraged too. Before I close this lesson, I want to encourage you in the area of holiness. Here is a passage that brings me great hope. Notice the phrase that begins the quote.

"**Because we have these promises**, dear friends, let us cleanse ourselves from everything that can defile our body or spirit. And let us work toward complete holiness because we fear God."
7 CORINTHIANS 7:1

Paul tells us that holiness is intricately related to "these" promises. A wise reader would ask, "What promises?" Looking back, you see the very promises Paul references. They are found in 2 Corinthians 6:16 to the end of the chapter:

> And what union can there be between God's temple and idols?
> For we are the temple of the living God. As God said:
>
> "I will live in them
>   and walk among them.
> I will be their God,
>   and they will be my people.
> Therefore, come out from among unbelievers,
>   and separate yourselves from them, says the Lord.
> Don't touch their filthy things,
>   and I will welcome you.
> And I will be your Father,
>   and you will be my sons and daughters,
>   says the Lord Almighty."

What are the promises that give us the power to pursue holiness? The first speaks of God living and walking among us. It refers to **His presence** in our lives. Because He is with us, living inside of us via the Holy Spirit, we have supernatural power to overcome sin.

The second promise is described in the same verse. It refers to **God's authority**. When we are completely His, He has the power and authority to deliver us from every evil. We can ask God, as Jesus instructed, to powerfully deliver us from the temptations and struggles which threaten our progress toward holiness.

The third promise is found at the end of the passage. Here Paul assures us that we have the promise of **intimacy with God**. Though God is King of the Universe, He is also our Daddy God, and, as Jesus declares our friend. In this promise of intimate relationship, we can trust Him, speak to Him, and listen to His wise advice. In these promises—God's presence, God's authority, and God's intimacy—we have everything we need to overcome sin and pursue holiness. Walking with Jesus, you will change!

Your Sex

Principle Number Five
God cares about your sexual relationship with y
because the sexual relationship plays an integral role in
human family.

Looking at our culture, you might conclude that the only reason for human sexuality is pleasure. And, while pleasure is certainly a part of God's plan for our sexuality, it was by no means his only intent. In fact, our designer had other ideas in mind. Look at this passsage from 1 Corinthians 7:3–5:

> The husband should fulfill his marital duty to his wife, and likewise the wife to her husband. The wife does not have authority over her own body but yields it to her husband. In the same way, the husband does not have authority over his own body but yields it to his wife. Do not deprive each other except perhaps by mutual consent and for a time, so that you may devote yourselves to prayer. Then come together again so that Satan will not tempt you because of your lack of self-control.

This passage tells us that the committed and vital sexual relationship between husband and wife protects the family. Paul gives us two principles that amplify that protective purpose.

In the first, Paul warns his readers that there is much sexual immorality in the world. We certainly understand that concept. Our world is rife with immorality. Even our leaders struggle. Bill Clinton, Tiger Woods and General David Patreaus have suffered the consequences. As hard as it is to imagine, it's possible that Paul's generation faced even more sexual immorality.

In Paul's day, pagan worship involved temple prostitutes, both women and men providing sex as a part of idol worship. In the city of Ephesus directions to public prostitutes were carved directly into the marble blocks of sidewalks. Prostitution was so much a part of Ephesian life that a public tunnel was built under the street between the main library and the public brothel. Ephesian men could enter the library, proceed downstairs and through the tunnel to the brothel. In Paul's time, Roman society expected men to have mistresses; wives were for procreation and family appearances only.

When I visited Pompeii, I was surprised to see depictions of aberrant sexual behaviors painted as murals in the houses of the city. Penises, carved into sidewalks, gave directions to brothels. No wonder Paul wanted to protect believers!

In the face of this kind of immorality, Paul had a second point to make. He reminds us that our bodies belong to our spouses, not to ourselves. These days, some might find this concept incredibly old fashioned, especially in a culture where independence and self-determination are so highly valued. But Paul shows us that one of our sexual purposes is to serve our spouse by meeting his sexual needs. The result of this is simple: By doing this one thing, we help our spouses to avoid sexual temptation.

Perhaps you've heard it implied that men only stray sexually when they aren't "getting any" at home. This oversimplification of adultery serves no useful purpose—other than to blame infidelity on the one betrayed. In truth, all of us face temptation. We don't have to give in. When adultery occurs, the responsibility lies primarily with the one who has strayed.

Yet, the Corinthian passage reminds us that when we meet our spouse's needs, we protect them from the temptation of sexual sin. Thus we protect our kids from the distress of broken trust, from the wounds of a broken marriage, and from the distraction of cataclysmic discord and unhappiness.

By keeping Paul's instructions, we model for our children the invaluable lessons of faithfulness and loyalty between a husband and wife. We show them that physical love can last a lifetime, in the same way that emotional, spiritual and friendship bonds will stand the test of time. **In the process of living sexually pure lives, we teach our children Godly values and set them up for success in their own marriage. In this way, we protect both our children and our grandchildren.**

The sexual relationship in marriage also provides for procreation. Clearly, God has a different view of children than many in our culture. There is no doubt, from many, many biblical passages, that God considers children to be one of His richest blessings— one that we should covet, receive and treasure with the greatest solemnity and gratitude. Consider, for now, these two passages:

> Children are a gift from the Lord; they are a reward from him.
> PSALM 127:3

> "The LORD will give you prosperity in the land he swore to your ancestors to give you, blessing you with many children, numerous livestock, and abundant crops."
> DEUTERONOMY 28:11

Though God's divine plan for the married sexual relationship includes blessing His people with children, this is not His only purpose. As a serious student of human anatomy, I have noticed that anywhere we look at the human body, design and function are inextricably linked. This is especially true when it comes to human sexuality.

In sexuality, human anatomy clearly shows us that pleasure is part of God's design. Let me give you just one example:

The human clitoris, part of a woman's external genitalia, has no anatomical function, other than pleasure. The thousands of nerve endings clustered in the clitoris give a woman intense pleasure during sexual arousal. Though some would argue that pleasure is part of the plan to encourage procreation, I disagree. The anatomy doesn't provide pleasure *only* when procreation occurs. Sexual arousal isn't pleasant only during the most fertile part of the menstrual cycle. Rather, pleasure is a continual part of the everyday design of human sexuality.

I wonder if God added pleasure to his design in order to strengthen the bond between husband and wife. By giving us this supremely pleasurable experience (as a writer who treasures words, I admit that nothing quite captures the magnitude of human orgasm.), and then restricting its use to marriage, God has designed a gift that we experience *only with our spouse*. No other human interaction has the power to give that level of delight, mutual attachment and release of tension.

This kind of pleasure pulls us back again and again to the one we love. Whether we are frustrated and unhappy, or experiencing the deepest marital satisfaction, sexual intercourse draws us together again. It demands that we work out our differences. It rewards us when we do. It gives us a secret, private pleasure that we share with no one else on earth. It belongs to the husband and wife alone.

God designed sexuality as a gift that protects our marriage, strengthens our bond, and blesses our families. It is a perfectly conceived plan. What a marvelous gift God has given his people. Have you celebrated the gift lately?

Time for Reflection

Have you told your spouse that you are reading this book?

Have you thanked him for his sexual gifts to you?

Would you consider asking him to pray for you during the course of your study?

This week, consider spending a moment every day giving thanks for God's sexual gift to you. Thank Him for His design, for His plan, for His goodness in choosing your spouse. Thank Him that He wants you to enjoy it. Then, ask Him for help in the specific areas that you feel are deficient. Ask Him to speak to you as you study. Ask Him for healing in your marriage, if you need it. Begin now to cover the next weeks in prayer as you anticipate the discoveries ahead! As you pray, write down the discoveries you make.

CHAPTER 2

The Power of Commitment

Most Christians understand that the Biblical standard for human sexuality can be declared in two simple sentences: One woman for one man. For Life.

The biblical command is clear. Unambiguous. Strict. Unflinching. The Bible allows no alternative variations of sexual conduct. Today, as you read these passages and study these principles, your past may come roaring back to haunt you. Please don't let old memories or regrets steal your future. None of us can go back and change our poor decisions (And we've all made poor decisions, believe me!) All of us must begin where we are. The future of your marriage depends both on understanding and living these divinely inspired principles. Now. Today. Trust Jesus to work these truths into your marriage.

In the book of Mark, Jesus himself preached this narrow viewpoint. Here is the full passage:

> Some Pharisees came and tried to trap him with this question: "Should a man be allowed to divorce his wife?"
>
> Jesus answered them with a question: "What did Moses say in the law about divorce?"
>
> "Well, he permitted it," they replied. "He said a man can give his wife a written notice of divorce and send her away."

> But Jesus responded, "He wrote this commandment only as a concession to your hard hearts. But 'God made them male and female' from the beginning of creation. 'This explains why a man leaves his father and mother and is joined to his wife, and the two are united into one.' Since they are no longer two but one, let no one split apart what God has joined together."
>
> Later, when he was alone with his disciples in the house, they brought up the subject again. He told them, "Whoever divorces his wife and marries someone else commits adultery against her. And if a woman divorces her husband and marries someone else, she commits adultery."
>
> MARK 10:2–12

Here Jesus explains why Mosaic law permitted divorce. It is clearly, according to Jesus, a matter of heart disease. Divorce happens when a man or woman allows his or her heart to harden. Certainly Jesus isn't holding one person responsible for the hardened heart of his or her spouse. Instead, over and over throughout the gospel accounts, Jesus repeats with stunning clarity that we believers are responsible only for the condition of our own hearts.

While most Christians understand the admonition against divorce, few are aware of Jesus' more restrictive instruction regarding re-marriage. The divorced believer is not to remarry, with two biblical exceptions.

You can read about it in Matthew 5:31, 32. Again, in this passage, from the famous Sermon on the Mount, Jesus is speaking.

> "You have heard the law that says, 'A man can divorce his wife by merely giving her a written notice of divorce.' But I say that a man who divorces his wife, unless she has been unfaithful, causes her to commit adultery. And anyone who marries a divorced woman also commits adultery."

According to Jesus, unfaithfulness is one condition where remarriage is permissable. Adultery on the part of one spouse allows the betrayed spouse to remarry. The other condition for remarriage is, of course, the death of the partner. Marriage vows extend only through the lifetime of both partners. Thus, when one of the partners dies, his spouse is free to remarry.

Paul gives us one other condition for remarriage. He approaches the subject in this passage:

> To the married I give this command (not I, but the Lord): A wife must not separate from her husband. But if she does, she must remain unmarried or else be reconciled to her husband. And a husband must not divorce his wife.
>
> To the rest I say this (I, not the Lord): If any brother has a wife who is not a believer and she is willing to live with him, he must not divorce her. And if a woman has a husband who is not a believer and he is willing to live with her, she must not divorce him. For the unbelieving husband has been sanctified through his wife, and the unbelieving wife has been sanctified through her believing husband. Otherwise your children would be unclean, but as it is, they are holy.
>
> But if the unbeliever leaves, let it be so. The brother or the sister is not bound in such circumstances; God has called us to live in peace.
> I CORINTHIANS 7:10-15

Paul allows those who are abandoned by their unbelieving spouse to remarry if they so wish. This is the third reason for remarriage.

I mention these passages not to bring condemnation, but to emphasize the incredible permanence of your marriage relationship. Divorce is serious; remarriage is, for the most part, forbidden. **If divorce and remarriage are part of your past, don't waste time in shame or regret. Instead, start fresh.**

If you haven't yet, ask God's forgiveness. If you need to, ask forgiveness of your former husband. As of today, recognize and fully

pursue the high standard God has for our sexual purity. Commit to it. Live that standard, with God's help, from this day forward.

Another well known marriage passage is found in the Old Testament book of Malachi. Most preaching on this passage focuses on God's hatred of divorce. However there is more here than meets the eye.

> You cry out, "Why doesn't the Lord accept my worship?" I'll tell you why! Because the Lord witnessed the vows you and your wife made when you were young. But you have been unfaithful to her, though she remained your faithful partner, the wife of your marriage vows.
>
> Didn't the Lord make you one with your wife? In body and spirit you are his. And what does he want? Godly children from your union. So guard your heart; remain loyal to the wife of your youth. "For I hate divorce!" says the Lord, the God of Israel. "To divorce your wife is to overwhelm her with cruelty," says the Lord of Heaven's Armies. "So guard your heart; do not be unfaithful to your wife."
>
> MALACHI 2:14–16.

Guard Your Heart and Remain Loyal

Malachi teaches us something both simple and profound about God's plan for marriage. God hates divorce; he wants our marrige to last. God has done more than simply witness our marriage vows, somehow in that sacrament, he has made two separate people into one. His deepest desire is that we remain in that relationship for life. Love or hate. Hot or cold. Grown apart or grown together. In peace or in anger. One man, one woman, for life. This passage gives us one other important insight. In the prophet's words, God gives us the antidote to divorce in two simple principles. You see them revealed in the last line of the passage:

1. **We are to guard our heart**
2. **We are to remain loyal to our spouse**

> **These two simple but demanding principles completely embody the message of this book.**

Years ago all wedding vows were essentially the same. Your grandparents and mine probably recited vows to one another using words like this, "I pledge thee my troth." Though the phrase is nearly meaningless to modern ears, in today's terms, it means, "I promise my faithfulness to you." The word troth comes from the same root as the word betrothal, and includes ideas like loyalty, faithfulness, and trust. It is almost the same concept God transmits through Malachi.

Today vows have changed. Many couples write their own wedding promises. But in nearly every case, during the exchange of promises, both parties commit themselves to an exclusive relationship using phrases like, "forsaking all others," or "I will love you alone."

The meaning remains the same. The husband and wife promise to live in a sexually exclusive relationship, giving themselves only to their spouse. This is a key part of the marriage pledge—this sexual promise made before witnesses. You promise your spouse, "I will not share myself with anyone else."

My pastor loves to quote his favorite marriage source when he officiates at weddings. The idea comes from the book T*he Mystery of Marriage*, by Mike Mason. Mason refers to the wedding vows as "wild promises," promises far too difficult for any human to keep outside of the constant support and dynamic power of a living God. Without God, most of us would fail miserably.

What enables believing couples to commit themselves exclusively to one another? Where does that kind of strength come from? Of course believers count on God's help to keep those wild promises. But they must also depend on another strategy. I believe that strength comes from the power of commitment.

Occasionally, you'll hear an older couple lament about today's sky rocketing divorce rate. "Young people just don't know how to commit these days," they say. But what does commitment really mean? Is it good enough to wear fancy clothes and make a public vow for a life-long, sexually exclusive relationship in front of family and friends? I don't think so.

As a young woman, I participated in competative gymnastics. In my small town we had no private gymnastics club. Everything I knew, I learned at school on improvised equipment. A teammate's father built our balance beam in his garage. A public school teacher served as our coach. The lack of expertise made for slow improvement.

When I arrived at the University of Washington, I was way out of my league. My teammates performed tricks I only imagined. My new coach demanded that I expand my skill set. Though I tried, I had one persistent flaw.

The first time I did any new skill, I flubbed it—not because I couldn't perform—but because it seemed that my eighteen-year-old brain couldn't make a commitment. I would run across the mat, start a tumbling run, progress through back handsprings and just as I reached the top of a back summersault, I backed out of the stunt.

Of course, in the middle of the air, when danger is at its height, there is no safe way to back out. The only way out is down. During these first attempts I usually landed in a heap directly on top of my spotter. Needless to say, my coach was horribly frustrated. It happened on the balance beam, on the uneven bars and even on the vault. I was a danger to myself and to my coach. The problem? I wasn't all in. I'd made a commitment I refused to keep. When the fear got big enough, I backed out.

Faithfulness in marriage and success in gymnastics take exactly the same kind of commitment. You must be all in. All of your energy, all of your strength, all of your attention must be focused on the task. You can't bail at the top of a back summersault and expect to survive. Neither can you make wild promises of faithfulness to your spouse with the secret hope of holding anything back.

When the fear hits it's zenith, you must be all in.

Compare this to the woman who once told me, "I knew—standing at the altar—that I would divorce my husband. I knew it was a mistake. On my wedding night divorce was all I could think of." I ask you, did her marriage stand any chance at all?

Time for Reflection

Write what you remember of your vows here:

What did you think would be the hardest part of keeping your vows? Were you right?

Keeping those wedding vows takes all your strength. To keep your wild wedding promises, you must be "all in" in every area of your marriage. How do you think that plays out in the area of sexual purity? Can you give examples?

The Meaning of Commitment

Does being "all in" mean simply that you manage to avoid having a sexual affair? If your husband told you that he was "all in," but admitted holding hands with a woman at work, sexting, or spending hours every day talking by telephone with another woman, would you consider him "all in?" Probably not. **Being sexually committed means that we will enjoy every aspect of our sexu-**

ality ONLY in the context of our exclusive relationship with our spouse. Anything else with anyone other than our spouse is unacceptable.

Most people believe that their wedding vows are enough to keep them from falling into sinful sexual relationships. But few understand that being "all in" involves decisions that you make every day. Let's develop this concept. Begin by trying to list all the ways that you share your sexuality with your spouse. For the time being, do not include the act of sexual intercourse:

Though your list may look slightly different, in its most basic terms you share yourself:

- Visually: (You expose yourself to your spouse)
- Verbally: (You speak about your sexual needs)
- Familiarity: (Because of your shared past and experiences)
- With Touch: (You touch one another in sexual ways)
- In your thoughts: (You think about one another sexually)
- Your sexual past: (You reveal past failures and experiences)
- Your sexual future: (Your desires, hopes, and dreams)

If you and your spouse share yourselves sexually in all of these different ways, isn't it also true that your decision to be faithful to your spouse will affect all of these same areas? If you want your sexual relationship to exclude others and bless ONLY your spouse, then you must support that choice over and over again as you proceed through your day.

In fact, the more you commit to the idea of sexual exclusiveness, the more opportunities you will find to turn your thoughts, your body, your actions, your choices toward your spouse alone.

In a later chapter, we'll use this same list to discover the many exciting ways that we can amp up the pleasure we experience in our married sexual relationship. Look back at the list. Each of these avenues of shared sexuality represents an important opportunity for growing intimacy with the one we love.

Time for Reflection

I know you've had it happen. An inappropriate compliment from a stranger, a "joke" from a coworker, suggestive, yet somehow vaguely affirming. As honestly as you can, describe how it feels when a man, other than your husband, whistles at you, or gives you some other form of sexual approval. Do you think your response is normal? Healthy? Godly?

When that happens, do you do anything to correct that person? What? What keeps you from speaking out? Should you? Always?

Visual Purity
As we think about the way we share ourselves visually, I'd like to use just one example to help you see how daily decisions reflect your commitment to sexual purity.

Your spouse is the only one who sees and knows every nook and cranny of your body. He knows your breasts, your skin, your curves. He knows your moles, your freckles, your birthmarks. Believe me, he delights in them. When he is enjoying your body, he does not take note of rolls or dimples. He does not care about the perkiness of your breasts or the thickness of your ankles. Most healthy husbands wouldn't begin to diagnose their wive's thighs as too big, or her tummy as doughy. For your spouse, your body is an oasis of viewing pleasure.

In his book, *Sheet Music*, Dr. Kevin Lehman (married 44 years) frankly confesses his continued delight in seeing his wife's breasts showing through the sheer fabric of lingerie when they are alone together. Despite the changes of aging, viewing her body gives him great pleasure, even many, many years after his wedding day.

Of course Dr. Lehman isn't unusual. The same is true for most men. If that were not so, most "skin" magazines like Playboy and Penthouse would find themselves out of business. Generally, women understand that men are visually aroused. Did you know that the difference has a biological basis? A recent article in *Biology of Sex Differences* states that **the visual cortex of men and women is significantly different, with men having 25 % more neurons than women** (http://www.medicalnewstoday.com/articles/249844.php).

During the course of a normal evening, your husband may be enticed by something as simple as watching your back as you load the dishwasher. (That may explain why he so seldom helps—he's having his own little party back there!) My point? If we can agree that men (for the most part) are visually aroused, then our commitment to sexual exclusivity should influence how we choose to let other men view our bodies. Our commitment to our spouse should include a commitment to dress publicly in ways that are not sexually suggestive to other men.

The problem is that for some women, using our body's sexual allure feels powerful. We have come to realize that our sexual attractiveness can be exchanged for advantage, attention, or advancement in the workplace. Using our sexual power may even extend beyond the workplace. We may use it to manipulate, to tease, or to influence men in our community or even our church.

In this way, our past hurts and beliefs (for instance, believing *the only reason anyone pays attention to me is because of my sexy body*) as well as the expectations of our culture (*I have to dress this way if I want that promotion*) continue to influence our present.

Those advantages may make us reluctant to choose a different path. Insecurity may lead us to wonder if we could make it on our own, without sexual manipulation. **The truth is this: if you must use sexual allure to succeed in your world, the price is too high.**

One day, as I drove home from my in-laws, I stopped for coffee at a roadside latte stand. The barista greeted me at the window dressed only in a black thong and a lacy bra. Shocked, I stammered, "I wouldn't have stopped here if I'd known."

"Oh, it's no problem," she said, smiling as if my complete surprise were a normal part of her workday. She was a beautiful young woman, with flawless skin and a perfect figure. For a moment, I envied her. Then, I began to feel the Holy Spirit speaking to me. I ordered a drink and gave myself time to think about what I was sensing.

When she returned, I said something along these lines. "You know, you don't have to sell your body like this. Your creator loves you so much. He thinks you are beautiful as a person, not just as a body. You don't have to work in scanty clothes in order to succeed." I worried that my awkward message would drive her away. Instead, she let me tell her the story of a woman I know.

This woman has been married three times. All three of her husbands have been abusive and controlling. She told me that one actually made her stand on a scale every day so that he could see if she had gained any weight. The common denominator in this succession of men was the way this woman chose to dress. When single, she consistently chose provocative clothing—partially exposed breasts and short, tight skirts. She was meticulous in her makeup and hair. To me it seemed she used her body to initiate relationships with men, like bait attracts fish.

Her clothing sent messages which did not match the intention and desires of her heart. In the end, she was confused about why she consistently attracted men who didn't care about who she was on the inside. Instead, she was approached only by men who focused on her sexuality. They did not care for her soul. While there were undoubtedly numerous other factors at work, her clothing did her no favors.

Our ability to use our sexuality in our interaction with the men around us is a two-edged sword. In the privacy of our homes, we can dress provocatively for our husbands and bring great pleasure to the one we love. But when we dress provocatively in the workplace and in the world we send a mixed message—one which betrays our deepest desire to be valued and respected as an individual with skills and talents beyond the shape of our body.

Women tell me they want the freedom to dress in any way they choose. Afterward, when their clothing choices have undesired consequences, they express frustration toward men. Sometimes I want to tell young women, "If you don't want him to stare at your breasts, don't expose them!"

There is certainly one other point of view worth considering. What does your husband think? How does he feel knowing that your clothing choices have a sexual effect on the men around you? Of course, he wants to feel proud of the beautiful woman he married, but is there something else? What if other men were aroused by your clothing? How would your husband feel?

And, what if the tables were turned? Would you want your husband to touch another woman in ways that cause her to be sexually aroused? Of course not! You would want him to save all of his sexual affection for you. You want exclusivity in the realm of sexual touch. Perhaps your husband wants the same visual exclusivity for you!

I'm not advocating that you dress in ugly, ill fitting, or out-of-style clothes. Our clothes provide a great way to express our personality, our skills—even our cultural relevance. Instead, I'm asking you to view your clothing as a direct expression of the sexual commitment you have made to your spouse. If we commit to visual exclusivity, we'll find ourselves asking important questions like these:

- What styles will I wear?
- What fabrics will I choose?
- What will I wear under those fabrics?
- How much skin will I show?
- How much cleavage will I expose?
- How short will I wear my dresses and skirts?

This issue isn't new. The Apostle Paul was concerned enough to give specific instructions to Timothy—a young and less experienced pastor—about how to handle these very questions:

> And I want women to be modest in their appearance. They should wear decent and appropriate clothing and not draw attention to themselves by the way they fix their hair or by wearing gold or pearls or expensive clothes.
> 1 TIMOTHY 2:9

Paul insists that women be recognized not by how they adorned their bodies, but rather by how they live their lives. It is character that counts, Paul emphasizes, not decoration. Paul didn't want the people in Timothy's congregation to be so distracted by outward appearances that they neglected the most important thing, the growth of character.

I can think of three Old Testament examples where sexual sin is preceded by this kind of visual attention. In all three cases, the course of biblical history is changed by what follows. The most obvious occurs after King David, gazing from his rooftop patio, views a woman bathing. Here is the passage:

> In the spring of the year, when kings normally go out to war, David sent Joab and the Israelite army to fight the Ammonites. They destroyed the Ammonite army and laid siege to the city of Rabbah. However, David stayed behind in Jerusalem.
>
> Late one afternoon, after his midday rest, David got out of bed and was walking on the roof of the palace. As he looked out over the city, he noticed a woman of unusual beauty taking a bath. He sent someone to find out who she was, and he was told, "She is Bathsheba, the daughter of Eliam and the wife of Uriah the Hittite." Then David sent messengers to get her; and when she came to the palace, he slept with her. She had just completed the purification rites after having her menstrual period. Then she returned home. Later, when Bathsheba discovered that she was pregnant, she sent a message to inform David.
> 2 SAMUEL 11:1-5

Without laying blame on Bathsheba (after all, she was only taking a bath in a way that was common to her culture), we can be certain that it was David's sexual response to what he saw that led to his pursuit, his adultery and eventually to the murder of Bathsheba's husband. The same visual stimulation occurs in the case of Dinah (Genesis 34) which led to rape, and of Samson (Judges 14) which led to a sinful marriage between an Israelite judge and a Philistine woman.

Since it is true that men are visually aroused, we women can express love to men around us by making careful, thoughtful clothing choices. **When you commit to modesty, you may actually protect the men around you from sexual sin.**

Let me be clear. Modesty need not be frumpy. Frumpy frequently has the same motivation as ostentatious ornamentation—in that it calls attention to itself. In some ways frumpy is a prideful declaration of false modesty. Modesty doesn't have to ignore fashion. It need not be unflattering. **Modesty simply chooses to avoid clothing which might stimulate a visual sexual response in men other than your husband.**

Time for Reflection

> Let no one say when he is tempted, "I am being tempted by God"; for God cannot be tempted by evil, and He Himself does not tempt anyone. But each one is tempted when he is carried away and enticed by his own lust. Then when lust has conceived, it gives birth to sin; and when sin is accomplished, it brings forth death. Do not be deceived, my beloved brethren.
> JAMES 1:13-16 NASB

From this passage, what three steps lead to death?

The NASB uses the word "lust." What do you think about when you hear the word lust? What is involved in lust? Can you define it?

If you were doomed to wear shapeless, frumpy, ugly clothes for the rest of your life, how would you feel? What does your response tell you about your relationship with clothes? What about your relationship with the approval and attractiveness that clothes may provide?

Pure Sex, Great Sex

Have you ever worn something especially revealing in the privacy of your husband/wife time? How did your husband react? How did that make you feel?

After you watch some Hollywood star play the part of an over-muscled battle weary warrior, how does your husband's body look to you? Can he compete with the lean, personally trained, professionally fed body of someone whose only job is to look "ripped?" My hardworking, sit-down-all-day-at-work husband certainly can't. Would you consider limiting your exposure to those kinds of images? How might you begin?

My Choice
I admit that I have difficulty watching films depicting other couples having sex. I find that those scenes stick to my brain, and can unexpectedly replay themselves at any time, even when I least expect. Unfortunately, I forget that I have been watching actors *portraying* a sex act. I find myself struggling with comparisons. Do I look as beautiful as she does? Does my husband enjoy me as much as that man enjoys that woman? Why aren't our moments together filled that kind of hot passion?

I forget that Hollywood doesn't focus on truth. Passion isn't always sweaty and aggressive. Sometimes passion—especially after many years in a committed relationship—is playful, light, tender and gentle. Sometimes passion is quiet, soft, and relaxing.

For that reason, I choose to avoid movies with sexual depictions. When I inadvertently find myself in front of a scene like that, I turn away or excuse myself for a moment. I don't want to compare what I share with my husband with some Hollywood illusion.

What about Pornography?
There is no question that the world has begun to accept pornography as a reasonable way to hype libido in a marriage relationship gone stale. Contemporary television laughs about it. In one episode of the hit sitcom "Friends," the Monica Geller character gives her new husband Chandler a porn tape for Valentines day. While that episode produced the expected laughs it also marked pornography as a "healthy" option for married sexuality.

Not long ago the question of pornography would not arise in a study of purity. Today however, nearly every aspect of worldly sexuality has a proponent in the "Christian" discussion. I have read online posts of Christians who proclaim that sado-masochism is their version of normal sexuality. You'll find the following comment on the Christianity Today website in response to an article by Jonalyn Fincher (discussing the 50 Shades books). This quote actually moved me toward writing this book. (The He here refers to God). Here is the quote:

> "He made me sadistic, He made my wife masochistic, and He made sure we got together despite the fact that neither of us were aware of that. We use his gifts to make sure we *stay* together." I'm "active" in the fetish community. I attend meetings in public locations (dinners, for the most part), and every once in a while I'll attend a private event (generally to see a seminar and/or learn or discuss a technique)."

I cannot tell you how much this comment baffled me. How can anyone view sadomasochism as an expression of godly married sexual love? As so many worldly expressions of sex invade the church, pornography has become a critical addiction among belivers. Consider these words, penned by porn addict Michael Leahy in his book *Porn Nation*:

> At this point in my life, I had become totally self absorbed. Patty and I were acting more like roommates than husband and wife. I was spending little time with either her or my boys as I was consumed with trying to manage the unmanageable. There was little intimacy left in our marriage, and our relationship revolved around accomplishing the every day tasks of running a family, of which she now carried the bulk of the burden. My sexual acting out behaviors were getting riskier and riskier, as simply viewing porn didn't do it for me any more. I started to spend more time fantasizing about being with other women, with real women, and started obsessing about having an affair. (Northfield Publishing, 2008, page 62)

Consider these statistics, provided by United Families International (unitedfamiliesinternational.wordpress.com)
- U.S. pornography revenue: $ 2.84 billion per year.
- Pornographic websites worldwide: 4.9 million (12% of total websites).
- Daily pornographic search engine requests: 68 million (25% of total search engine requests).
- Daily pornographic e-mails: 2.5 billion (8% of total e-mails).
- U.S. adults who regularly visit Internet pornography web sites: 40 million.
- 20% of men admit viewing Internet porn at work.
- Every second 28,258 Internet users are viewing porn.

Pornography has not only invaded our society; it has invaded the church. Some experts estimate that half the men in any ordinary congregation regularly view porn. They also believe that 1 in 3 Christian men have symptoms of addiction. Addiction is not limited to the men in our congregation. Focus on the Family has reported a steady increase in the number of pastors seeking help for pornography addiction as well.

Certainly, pornography is titillating. It heightens sexual awareness and might lead to a temporary increase in passion. But where else might it lead? I'll give you specific answers to that question in our last chapter. But for now, consider this:

When a couple views pornography together a woman allows another woman into her bedroom. She allows her husband to be stimulated and sexually aroused by other women. It opens a woman's intimate behavior to comparison. Who can compete with the artificial depictions created on a sound stage? Pornography wreaks havoc with the exclusive sexual relationship between a man and a woman. When occasional use becomes addiction, pornography can also destroy your man. Frequently, it destroys a marriage and family. It may even destroy you. Men are not the only ones who experience pornography addiction.

Pornography also has unexpected consequences. In fact, most experts treating porn addicts would agree that pornography swiftly moves from an occasional viewing to an obsession that begins to haunt every aspect of normal life. The addict moves quickly from observer to participant in potentially dangerous behaviors—watching child porn, participating in anonymous sex at bookstores, random affairs, prostitution and more.

Pornography has other power as well. When it becomes addictive, the remaining partner is excluded, often feeling either used or abandoned. In the 2002 report by the American Academy of Matrimonial Lawyers, compulsive Internet use played a significant role in divorces, with well over 50% of those cases involving pornography. (*The Essential Guide to Overcoming Problems Caused by Pornography*, Harper Collins, 2010, page 3) **Pornography does not promote intimacy with one's spouse; instead, it promotes intimacy with pornography. It focuses on the use of toys, positions, techniques—not on growing closer together through the giving and receiving of sexual pleasure.** No wonder the addict's partner feels left out.

I have heard of one addict who confessed, "After using porn, I lost my ability to tell right from wrong. It was as if my 'sin sensor' had died in the process." The death of your conscience is a very high price to pay.

Pornography is a poison infiltrating and destroying God's sexual gift to husbands and wives. In the process, it may destroy the family as well.

Of course, the pornography industry uses and abuses people. Pornography is an industry which defies every Godly value. It demeans women by reducing them to sexual objects, abuses children, and encourages adultery and fornication. It prospers in the darkest parts of the human heart, and in the dark alleys of our cities. It has fostered the staggering growth of an entire sex trade industry. It is a money-maker for criminals and organized crime. Why would a godly couple want to participate?

If your husband is encouraging you to give pornography a try, I encourage you to consider these issues. In the clear light of day, when your emotions and hormones are under complete control, bring your concerns to your husband. Tell him that you want, more than anything, to enjoy a completely uninhibited and gratifying sexual life with him. Be sure that he understands that you desire to "light his fire." Then, explain that you have reservations about using pornography to do so.

If you need to, ask him to talk about his desires together with the help of a trained counselor. If that seems too difficult, consider having coffee as a couple with someone who has struggled with a pornography addiction. Talk about your concerns openly and ask for this person's perspective on the journey he or she has experienced.

Consider too that your husband may already be involved with pornography. By bringing you into his compulsion, he may be attempting to "normalize" his behavior. Don't be afraid to ask hard questions. Get the support you need to deal with his answers. Above all, don't give up hope.

Like all addictions, pornography addiction is treatable. If your husband uses pornography, and you are worried, get help for yourself. Many churches provide groups for the spouses of addicts. Join one.

In today's world, both women and men are finding themselves trapped in pornography's unrelenting grip. **Women can become addicted to pornographic material just as men can. If you are addicted, begin by telling someone you trust the whole truth about your situation. This addiction gains power in secrecy and shame.**

If you discover yourself caught in this web, confess. Ask for help. Take all the necessary steps to take back your life! Jesus died so that you could be fully free from the power of sin. Walk toward that freedom; the enemy will tell you it is hopeless. Don't believe his evil lie.

No one can kick the habit alone. The harder you try, the more likely you are to see yourself as weak, and your situation as hopeless. Some even give in to suicide. Don't give up. Get help. In Jesus, there is always hope.

Are there ways other than pornography to generate heat in the bedroom? Yes, absolutely. We'll talk more about that in later chapters!

Over the next week, I'd like you to focus on the idea of sexual exclusivity. Begin to take note of the ways you share yourself sexually with your spouse. These will include many behaviors other than intercourse. As you think about them, write them down. Think about how you keep those behaviors limited exclusively to your spouse. Consider how you might protect those behaviors from being shared with others. Here again is my list (though yours may be different):

Visually: (You expose yourself to your spouse)
Verbally: (You speak about your sexual needs)
Familiarity: (Your shared sexual past and experiences)
With Touch: (You are free to touch one another in sexual ways)
In your thoughts: (You think about one another sexually)
Your sexual past: (You reveal your past failures and experiences)
Your sexual future: (Your hopes desires and dreams)

This week, pay attention to television, magazine and media depictions of sexuality. Cut out ads and pictures, write down stories or headlines that tell a story or make a promise that is not in line with God's view of sexuality.

I've included space for you to record your thoughts below.

Clearing the Garden

My brother-in-law, an electrician, is a gentleman farmer. Every fall, he preserves his garden bounty, lining shelves with jars of beans, tomatoes, pickles, corn, fruits and other vegetables. Dan's abundance is no accident. It comes from early planning and hard work. Every spring, Dan heads out to his fenced garden plot and plows it under. Then, as rotting grasses enrich the soil, Dan plans his summer crops. Eventually, when the time is perfect, when the rain has stopped and all sign of frost ends, he plants. In the fall, his hard work pays off. Lucky for me, Dan loves to share.

At this point, three chapters into our study, you might begin to think that I'm planning to focus only on restrictions. It might even begin to feel as though I'm spending all our time pointing my index finger at you, warning you away from everything you enjoy about our culture.

That's not my plan.

Instead, like my brother-in-law Dan, I'm planning ahead for a fruitful crop. Soon, very soon, we'll plant the seeds of a healthy sexual relationship in your marriage. We'll fertilize what grows well. But before we get there, we must spend time removing the weeds and debris from the past, plowing it under so that it fertilizes the good things yet to grow. Be patient with me, my friend.

We won't be much longer.

This week, we'll look at other ways women betray the exclusive relationship they have promised in their wedding vows. I'm not accusing you of adultery. I'm simply going to ask you to think of ways that you may bring expectations, desires, imaginations and yes, even other people into your sexual relationship with your husband. At times our discussion may make you uncomfortable. It may even hurt. But I promise, if you'll stick with me, we can clear the soil of your sexual garden, so that a fruitful relationship can grow where weeds once choked the soil.

Only through careful introspection and application can we follow Soloman's admonition:

> Drink water from your own well—share your love only with your wife. Why spill the water of your springs in public, having sex with just anyone? You should reserve it for yourselves. Don't share it with strangers. Let your wife be a fountain of blessing for you. Rejoice in the wife of your youth. She is a loving deer, a graceful doe. Let her breasts satisfy you always. May you always be captivated by her love. Why be captivated, my son, by an immoral woman, or fondle the breasts of a promiscuous woman?
>
> PROVERBS 5: 15–20

In chapter two, we considered two important points. The first was commitment. In order to have a rewarding and fulfilling sex life, you must fully commit to a sexually exclusive relationship with your spouse. Next, we applied that exclusivity to our visual life, considering how exclusivity might affect our choices in clothing, in movies, and finally, in consideration of pornography.

In this chapter, we're going to continue thinking about how our sexually exclusive relationship might affect our choices. In the process,

I will give you advice which will undoubtedly clash with society's beliefs. I may even confront some of your own deeply held opinions.

My best friend, a man?
In our culture, the very concept of exclusivity is under assault. I'm not talking about what we've come to describe as serially monogamous relationships—where people take one lover after another throughout their lifetime. Most believers know better. They understand God's vision of marriage as a single life-long relationship. Instead, I'm talking about something much more subtle.

I'm talking about women having men as their "best friends."

We see it in movies, where women serve as best man for their "best friend's" wedding, or women who have male bridesmaids or their closest love-advisors are men. On Oprah, women defend their right to have male "best friends," despite the objections or sometimes even with the support of their husbands. (I assure you; Oprah isn't the place to stock up on godly wisdom.)

At the risk of being prudish, I'll tell you this truth: To consider a man (not your husband) as your best friend is the most dangerous thing any married woman can do. It isn't that a man cannot be a friend; he can. Men understand friendship; they bond and support one another in ways most women do not understand. I maintain that **a man cannot safely be the best friend of a married woman. Such a relationship, no matter how innocently it begins, will undermine your marriage.** It may even destroy it.

I've seen it happen, time and time again. Here is how it goes: The friendship begins innocently enough. The two of you have something in common—hobbies, interests, work, volunteer opportunities. You spend time with your friend. Your husband may even know and approve of the relationship. You share your inner world with your friend. Eventually, perhaps without meaning to, you expose your husband's weaknesses. (What husband doesn't have weaknesses? What wife doesn't share her frustrations and misunderstandings with her friends?) He responds by taking your side (as best friends do).

Now your friend has become your husband's adversary. As you and your friend grow more intimate (emotionally), your friend's innocent touches take on addditional meaning. A hug lingers. His hand brushes your hair away. He puts his hand over yours as you order lunch. He touches the small of your back as you cross the street. Short conversations become longer, more deeply intimate. He begins to affirm you in ways your husband no longer does. The touches grow more frequent, more exciting. Eventually, one of you crosses a boundary and what began as a friendship has grown into adultery.

I watched it happen with an author I know, with a mother from our children's elementary school, with a female music teacher, and with a dental hygienist. **In my 38 years of marriage, I've lost count of the numbers of marriages destroyed on the rocks of a "*safe* best-friend relationship with a man."**

There may be such a thing. But I have never once observed it.

Knowing this as I do, I've chosen to put tight restrictions on my relationships with men. Let me give you some examples. In 2002, when I co-wrote a book with author Chuck Dean, we put very clear boundaries around our writing collaboration. Both Chuck and I were committed to sexual purity. Aware of the difficulty, we agreed to work together entirely over the Internet. We limited the intimacy of our electronic conversations. In the entire course of writing the book, we met only once, when our book was finished. In a bookstore surrounded by scores of people, we exchanged the disk containing our text. Yes, we did drink coffee.

As I watch young women today, I'm aware of how easy it is to begin and continue an electronic friendship with a man. Old friends contact us via Facebook. We share our email and cell phone numbers. One text becomes two. Two becomes twenty. Meeting for coffee, at the gym, or after school feels safe; after all, you are surrounded by people.

Even when such a friendship has crossed no physical boundaries, it has the potential to destroy the exclusive emotional intimacy of your marriage. Let me tell you a story:

One cold winter night, I left a meeting and headed to my car. In the dark parking lot, I discovered that I had parked near an old friend. I greeted her and asked how she was doing. I sensed something wrong, but she denied any difficulty. "You don't seem fine," I said.

Quietly she began to cry. Devastated, she shared only part of her story. I asked questions. Eventually she confessed that she had become deeply connected to a family friend. Though the relationship had never become physical, her heart was completely lost to this man. If he had asked her to leave her husband, I believe she would have considered it.

By an act of grace, this man had ended their relationship that very day. She did not know why and as far as I know, he never contacted her again. Though they never committed adultery—at least not in the physical sense—the damage was significant. My friend had gone through a death that would take years to heal. Her emotional devastation was palpable, and she could not lean on her husband to help her through her grief.

Who knows how that betrayal affected her marriage? Did she ever tell her husband? Should she? I don't know. I only know that with wisdom, her pain might have been avoided.

Though she publically committed to an exclusive relationship with her husband, she had not made the practical choices that would protect that relationship.

Only you can decide what practical choices might protect your marital intimacy. I know of one affair that occurred when Christian "friends" were asked (by their Christian company) to travel together for business. In that case, the friendship morphed into adultery in the environment of long trips together—trips that involved hours in airports, meals in hotel restaurants and eventually in the anonymity of cities where neither was accountable to anyone. Both marriages were destroyed. Both careers ended.

I know of another affair that developed in a church environment, where two people ministered in the same area. Long hours of collaboration developed into friendship and eventually into adultery. Both people abandoned their spouses and their children, quit their jobs, and moved together to another state. Remarkably, they obtained jobs working in a new church.

What practical steps might protect you in today's world? I would reconsider the safety of Facebook friendships, of texting, of emailing, of commuting, of coffee meetings, of work meetings alone with another man. I would be especially aware of any man to whom I felt any degree of physical or emotional attraction.

Attraction is not sin. Passivity about that attraction may lead to sin. Do you remember the key principles of this book? They came from Malachi. We are to remain loyal to our spouse and we are to guard our hearts. The issue of male friendship falls under the catagory of guarding our heart.

If you are faced with continued contact with someone you find attractive, begin immediately to protect your emotions. Try to limit your contact. Choose to work in environments where others are present. If you must commute with a man, invite another woman to travel with you. **Consider finding another job. If you are continually thrown in with someone you find especially attractive. Unemployment, no matter what the cost, is always cheaper than divorce.** In order to make these incredibly wise decisions, you must be very aware of your feelings, and at the same time, ruthlessly honest with yourself.

God honors these kinds of decisions; ask Joseph.

Time for Reflection

Take your time working through these questions. They may be painful, but don't skip over them. The answers to these questions may help you know if you are at risk for serious sexual temptation:

Do you find yourself thinking about another man outside of the time you spend together? Who? Why?

If you know you will see him, do you think about him as you dress, making choices about more flattering or revealing clothes based on seeing him? Do you work harder to be attractive when you know he will be present?

When you are with your husband, do you think about this other man? Do you compare your husband to this man?

When you compare this man to your husband, does your husband come up "short?"

If you answered yes to any of these questions, consider your answer to be an early warning system. Take action now. In spite of what the culture tells us, our feelings are under our own control. Reign them in before it's too late.

Physical Attraction Isn't Sin
So, what do you do? Here are some practical suggestions:

When you feel that physical attraction, tell a trusted Christian girlfriend immediately. Ask for accountability and prayer. Ask your girlfriend to help you brainstorm ways to protect your heart and your marriage. Consider telling your husband and asking him to help you think of ways around continued contact. His creativity might surprise you. His support may help you realize how much you have to lose. I know he will be happier to hear about your feelings before your attraction develops into something dangerous.

At the risk of embarrassing myself, let me give you another example. In the publishing world, I found myself working with a man that many other authors found very attractive. One of my friends told me that she was worried for me. "I don't think you should work with him," she said. "It's too dangerous."

Frankly, I wasn't worried. I didn't find him attractive in the same way. However, before I began work with him, I consulted my 'walking girls.' We four women, who all attend the same church, have been walking nearly every weekday for almost 25 years. They know me as well as anyone. "I don't sense any truth in this warning," I said. "So am I stupid? Should I back out?"

We discussed the dangers openly. I admitted my own emotional weaknesses. Like every human, I have an Achilles heel (or two)—ways that I am vulnerable to temptation. After much discussion, we agreed that I might continue to work with this man, ***if I would commit to honesty with my friends.*** They promised they would keep their antenna up, asking pointed questions if necessary. If at any time things looked suspect, they would call me to account. I have no doubt that they would.

That discussion happened five years ago. I am grateful that my relationship with this man has proven both safe and fruitful. You see, when you bring temptation into the light, as I did with my closest companions, temptation loses much of its power.

Another Man in Another Form?
Not every "other man" is someone you know. Some live on the pages of romantic novels. Some inhabit the villages of television soap operas.

Sometimes, as you begin to remove the weeds, you will find additional weeds in the most unusual places. Don't be afraid to pluck them up and throw them out. Your marriage will be better because of your courage. And by the way, **your** weeds may not be at all like anyone else's. Don't be afraid to take care of your own issues. The Holy Spirit is faithful to show them to us, as He was when He instructed me to end my daytime soap viewing!

Ask the Lord's help as you consider how your choices might undermine your husband's place in your thought life. It might be time to make changes, to consider other reading material, or to turn off certain programing. I know of one women who recognized that romance novels had become especially dangerous for her. She determined never to read another. Pray first to be willing. Then listen carefully for the Holy Spirit.

The Man of Your Dreams: Controling your Mind
Here are the inner thoughts of a woman in a very "hot" love relationship. They are found in the Song of Solomon. Pay attention to this woman's words about her husband. . .

> My lover is dark and dazzling, better than ten thousand others! His head is the finest gold, and his hair is wavy and black. His eyes are like doves beside brooks of water, they are set like jewels. . . His body is like bright ivory, aglow with sapphires. His legs are like pillars of marble set in sockets of the finest gold, strong as the cedars of Lebanon. Non can rival him. His mouth is altogether sweet. He is lovely in every way. Such o women of Jerusalem, is my lover, my friend.
> SONG OF SONGS 5: 10–16

This bride has chosen to focus her thoughts on her husband. In the Song of Solomon text, you can see that her husband isn't perfect. He's frequently absent, frequently obsessed with his work. Sound familiar? Yet go back and look at her words. None of her frustrations peek through her description of him. This bride is a very wise woman. (We'll look at this passage again in chapter seven). We know that the human mind is a powerful tool. Using these techniques, people harness the power of the mind to achieve astounding accomplishments. You've used them too:

- Setting goals
- Performance focus
- Eliminating distractions
- Guided imagery
- Progress review
- Adjusted approach based on results

Though successful people certainly work at their skills in the real world, athletes, entrepreneurs, investors, even ministry executives use mental focus to create the reality they hope to achieve.

Used positively, the mind has the power to move us toward our goals. However, the mind also has the power to keep us anchored in the past, or mired in the present. It can prevent us from finding freedom from addictions or hurts. It can move a dissatisfied heart toward sadness, turn disappointment into bitterness and grow frustration into rage. **Your thought life determines the course of your emotions and ultimately the course of your actions.**

We see this principle illustrated in hundreds of passages of scripture, where a single thought takes root in the human mind and grows into sin. Consider Haman in the book of Esther, who allowed his hatred for Mordecai to fester into a murder plot against all Jews. Consider Joseph's brothers (Genesis 37), who let envy develop into a conspiracy to kill their younger brother. Consider Absalom who let his father's rejection ferment until he planned a deliberate political coup (2 Samuel 15).

In ways large and small, our thought life has the power to change our world. How we think. What we think. What we conclude about our world. Our thought life leads our emotions and influences our relationships. Let me give you a simple example.

Though she almost never complains to me about her husband, my oldest daughter called recently, intensely frustrated by a conversation she'd had with Jeff. Molly was taking their newborn to a doctor's appointment when Jeff called. "I cleaned up the dining room," he said.

By the time she called me, she was fuming. "Why would he say that except to point out that I didn't clean up after lunch? I have a newborn. I'm doing the best I can. How can he be so critical?"

I thought for a minute. Poor Molly was exhausted; it had been weeks since she'd had a full night's sleep. Jeff was struggling to keep up with his work and help with the baby. I ventured some advice, "Maybe that isn't what he's saying at all. You know, he can't nurse the baby. He's no help in the middle of the night. But he can wash the dishes. Maybe he just wants to know that you appreciate his effort. Maybe it's his way of telling you that he's doing his best. Maybe all he really wants is to hear you say, 'Thanks.'"

For a long moment, Molly didn't answer. Then she said, "I guess that's one way of thinking about it." At the time, I don't think she bought my suggestion. But she'd gotten my point. **Sometimes, how you feel about what you experience depends on how you interpret it. Our thoughts do determine our feelings.**

So, in the garden of your sexual purity, you might want to consider your thought life. What thoughts do you let nest in your mind during the day? Are you thinking about a guy who works in your office? Are you letting critical thoughts about your husband run in endless loops while you pick up his dirty laundry? Are you letting comparisons with other husbands, or other men wear holes in your husband's value? Do you think about how much more sensitive your best friend's husband is? How much more spiritual your home group leader is? How much more fit is your tennis instructor?

What about past relationships? Do you compare your husband to past loves? Do you often wonder about the guy you *didn't* marry? Have you looked up an old flame on Facebook?

I'll confess. I've failed in this area. And I have a good friend who is kind enough to call me on my failure. About twenty years ago, my husband and I were going through a very rough patch. During that time, I found myself sitting at stop lights watching the guys who drove by, wondering what kind of husbands they might be. I found myself wondering why I was hurting so much. And wondering if loving someone else would hurt less.

As I often do, I made self-deprecating jokes about it. What I was thinking and feeling began to creep into my humor. I remember using phrases like, "my next husband." Though I wasn't really planning on a next husband, my pain had seeped into my conversation. During that time, a good friend invited me to a local street fair and something life-changing ensued. As nearly as I can remember, this is what happened:

We had trouble finding parking so she dropped me off on a street corner. Just as I closed the car door, she blurted out something like, "You know, Bette. I think you should stop talking that way about other men. You don't mean it, I know. But you shouldn't give it any room in your thoughts."

Even before she drove away I knew she was right. By allowing those ideas into my head and by giving them voice, I had allowed a sin seed to take root in my garden. Before she returned, I repented and began to take responsibility for the direction of my wayward thoughts.

Scripture tells us that our thought life is powerful and that our weapons to control our thoughts are supernatural! We can channel that power in whatever way we choose. I want always to choose purity, faithfulness and holiness.

Your thought life is much more ethereal than your reading list, movie, or texting habits. Because of that, monitoring it requires more focus and more honesty. It won't be easy, but in order to find weeds and remove them you must consider the ideas that dwell in your thought-life. I can't tell you exactly what your weeds will look like. But because you are as human as I am, you have weeds as well. Because you can't see them, you may need a friend.

Suppose that you discover thoughts that shouldn't hang around in your head. How do you banish them? It isn't as if you can put them in a bag and deliver them to the Goodwill. Here, scripture gives us great advice. Notice the connection between the thought life and behavior:

> With the Lord's authority I say this: Live no longer as the Gentiles do, for they are hopelessly confused. Their minds are full of darkness; they wander far from the life God gives because they have closed their minds and hardened their hearts against him. They have no sense of shame. They live for lustful pleasure and eagerly practice every kind of impurity.
>
> But that isn't what you learned about Christ. Since you have heard about Jesus and have learned the truth that comes from him, throw off your old sinful nature and your former way of life, which is corrupted by lust and deception. Instead, let the Spirit renew your thoughts and attitudes. Put on your new nature, created to be like God— truly righteous and holy.
>
> EPHESIANS 4:17–24

Have you ever had a song stick in your mind? Did you know that the best way to banish a cheesy song is to listen to different music? Before the end of the first chorus those irritating lyrics will have vanished. Both Ephesians and Colossians give us similar advice. They don't ask us to simply remove our old life. They ask us to replace it with a new and holy life.

 In the same way, we must replace our "weedy" thoughts with appreciative, holy thoughts. It isn't enough to try to "stop thinking" things. Instead we must give our minds something new to focus on, something as honorable and appreciative as the Shulamite woman in the Song of Solomon.

That choice will affect your sex life. **One of my walking friends said it this way, "You can't spend the day thinking about what a**

jerk your husband is and then expect to have great sex when he comes home at night." She's right!

Your thought life is a fruitful garden for sexual purity. Your thoughts can foster affection for your husband, appreciation for the man he is becoming, gratitude for God's kindness to you—as He expressed it in your husband—appreciation for your husband's gifts and talents, and for his love and protection. These are the things that must fill your thoughts as you replace the weeds in your mind.

This New Testament passage also amplifies the power of putting on new thoughts:

> So put to death the sinful, earthly things lurking within you. Have nothing to do with sexual immorality, impurity, lust, and evil desires. Don't be greedy, for a greedy person is an idolater, worshiping the things of this world. . . . Put on your new nature, and be renewed as you learn to know your Creator and become like him. . . Since God chose you to be the holy people he loves, you must clothe yourselves with tenderhearted mercy, kindness, humility, gentleness, and patience. Make allowance for each other's faults, and forgive anyone who offends you. Remember, the Lord forgave you, so you must forgive others. Above all, clothe yourselves with love, which binds us all together in perfect harmony.
> COLOSSIANS 3:5–14

No husband is perfect, yet by focusing on your spouse's good qualities you will reduce your mind's ability to gripe and complain and compare. Your mind cannot truly focus on two things at once—no matter how much you think you multi-task! Try it. Changing your thought patterns will make a difference in your feelings toward your husband.

When Weeds of the Past Overwhelm the Present
When I was a young bride, only foolish people thought about how our past experiences influenced our present. We covered horrible childhoods with glib phrases like, "They (our parents) did the best they could." We dismissed horrific abuse with Christianese application of scripture, "forgetting those things which are behind."

The end result of this kind of thinking was that we never considered how *what* we experienced influenced our ability to love freely and openly in the here and now. We never considered how our past pain might make us manipulative, or demanding, or controlling—all in an effort to avoid future pain. We never considered how the lack of love in our past might actually blind us to love in our present.

Certainly, to ignore the past is the easy way. It does not require us to remember, to feel the pain, to forgive those who hurt us, or even to consider the ways our own behavior may have played a part in what happened to us. Ignoring the past allows us to continue evil behavior while blaming others for our situation. Ignoring the past keeps us from the very freedom that enables us to live a new and different life.

Of course, our past includes more than our childhood. Our history may be littered with other sexual relationships, previous marriages, or even sexual abuse. These issues may also influence our relationship with our spouse. Consider this story:

A woman once told me that she had enjoyed premarital sex with her husband. All through her childhood, from parents and youth workers, she had heard this message: "An immoral woman will never have a happy marriage, or a fullfilling sexual relationship with their spouse." What my friend concluded was that an immoral woman didn't deserve to be happy. In her mind God's forgiveness didn't include restoration. Though she had repented of her sin, she experienced a miserable married sex life. It was many years before she understood that the message of her youth leader had invaded her relationship with her husband, convincing her of lies that kept her from the joy God intended.

In one grace-filled moment, she realized how that old message had stolen her present joy. Her past had influenced her present.

To ignore the past is to ignore the power of forgiveness.

We cannot completely cover the subject of healing in the course of this material. Still, I assure you that healing is possible. I am living proof. Forgiveness is possible. You can forgive others; you can forgive yourself. For most of us, this kind of healing doesn't happen overnight. It rarely happens without the experienced wisdom of a professional guide.

Christian therapy can make a tremendous difference in your ability to leave the past behind. I know. I've experienced that life change. Don't let excuses keep you from the healing you know you need. I encourage you to sacrifice in order to finance professional help. Work overtime. Trade babysitting. Sell your house. Steal time from your everyday life to do the work that must be done. The more horrific your past, the more critical is your need to pursue healing. Make it happen, whatever the cost.

What will it cost? Financially, most good therapy isn't free. This kind of therapy rarely happens in the ordinary pastor's office. Most pastors don't have time to do a thorough job. Most are not adequately trained. Most likely, you'll need a Christian professional with advanced training. (Some larger churches have well trained professional counselors on staff. These experts can guide your healing journey.)

In addition to therapy, you might consider other resources. Some churches provide opportunities for healing, or soaking prayer.

Some locations have group therapy for women working with similar issues. I encourage you to stay open to any available help. Above all, if you do not find healing, continue to seek and knock and ask for the help you need.

I must warn you. Therapy will cost you emotionally as well as financially. In order to forgive, you will have to assess the damage, to count the cost of the evil done against you. You will feel the pain again, perhaps for the first time. In the process, you'll discover God's hand in your past. You will see (in the case of abuse) your own innocence. You will, for the first time, begin to see the world as it is, instead of viewing everyone and everything through the lens of woundedness, abuse and shame.

This may be the first time you've considered therapy. Please don't dismiss the longing you have for a pain-free life. Pray about it. Pray about the financial commitment involved. Therapy can change your world view. From personal experience I can attest: the view is much better from this side of healing!

When Love Hunger Leaves You Vulnerable:
Sometimes our past, though not horrific, leaves us with an emptiness that makes us especially vulnerable. Sometimes, being human leaves us vulnerable. Consider these passages from Proverbs.

> So she seduced him with her pretty speech and enticed him with her flattery. He followed her at once, like an ox going to the slaughter. He was like a stag caught in a trap, awaiting the arrow that would pierce its heart.
> PROVERBS 7: 21

> Love wisdom like a sister; make insight a beloved member of your family. Let them protect you from an affair with an immoral woman, **from listening to the flattery** of a promiscuous woman.
> PROVERBS 7:4,5

While it's easy to understand how childhood abuse might leave a person starved for attention and love, other less obvious situations might also leave similar scars. **Imgine the love-hunger that might be experienced by the youngest child in a very large family. What about a little girl whose father was lost to war or violence? What about a little sister, whose big sister was stunningly beautiful?** Can you see how these situations might leave children vulnerable to the flattery and attention of adults other than their spouse?

When I was a little girl, parents weren't encouraged to express their love. My father's mantra was, "Children are to be seen and not heard." While he was physically present, he was emotionally absent. I grew up desperate for male attention. That vulnerability led me into many unhealthy relationships. I have considered my past and recognized my vulnerabilty. Perhaps you have a vulnerability of your own?

Time for reflection

Once, many years ago, a man separated me from a crowd at a party and filled my ears with pretty words. It was very effective. I nearly swooned. How about you? How easily are you influenced by compliments—about your work, about your appearance, about your character?

Have you ever observed a man who used "flattering speech" to influence others around him? What were the effects of his words?

When you were a child, were you frequently approved? Did you hear negative speech about you, your body, your intellect, your humor, your personality? How might those words have left you vulnerable to the unhealthy attention of others?

If your marriage is currently difficult, are you starved for the attention of a kind word?

Planting new thoughts: When you think about your husband, I'll bet you could easily list those qualities that make you crazy. It's time to replace those unhealthy thoughts. Begin by thinking about the qualities that made you fall in love with him in the first place. Consider those good qualities that you have discovered over the course of your marriage. In the space below, make a list of the healthy thoughts you can plant to replace the negative thoughts now growing in your emotional garden.

What gifts does your husband possess?

In what ways are you grateful for his love?

How is he a good parent?

How is he a good friend? A good provider? A hard worker?

What good qualities does he express in his daily life? His work?

How is he an inspiration to your Christian walk?

This next question is especially important. If you are studying in a group, be certain to discuss your response together. How do you know when a man—other than your spouse—appreciates you? What signals (both verbal and non-verbal) do you pick up?

How do you feel when you are appreciated (whether for performance, skills or looks)?

Have you ever consciously used your sexuality (the way you dress, walk, speak or behave) to manipulate other men? Describe what happened:

Again, if you are in a group, be certain to discuss this question: What does it mean to flirt? Do you? Where did you learn to do that? Does it gain you anything? How does it feel to flirt?

Why does sexuality have power? Why does it work?

How do you choose your clothes?

For whom do you dress?

Do you ever think about who will be present at your event as you choose your clothing? (This is a repeat of a prior question in a new context. Think again about your answer.)

In our culture people use the word "sexy" all the time. I've heard it describe everything from new cars to wedding dresses. What does the word mean to you? Is it overused? Or, is our culture over sexed?

Trading Sexuality for Favor:
I chose these questions for a reason. **Most of us are either unaware, or deny that we use our sexuality to gain favor in our world. The truth is more complex.** I admit that I've done it.

Once, more than thirty years ago, I rear-ended someone at a traffic light. The only casualties in the accident were my headlights. It happened after dark, and I had no lights to drive home. I bought new lights at a nearby auto parts store, and because I couldn't do it myself, went to a gas station to have them installed. The gas station attendant told me he wasn't allowed to do this kind of work.

Shamelessly, I flirted with him until he changed his mind. As I drove away with my new headlights, I heard the Holy Spirit say, "Don't ever do that again." I knew that by flirting, I had dealt fraudulently with the attendant. The Holy Spirit was disappointed in my behavior. I repented and promised to obey. At first that promise was hard to keep. Growing up without Christ, I had developed the habit of flirting in order to get my way. As a Christian that kind of manipulation saddens my Savior.

As women, we pick up on the signals men send us. We understand the meaning of prolonged eye contact, prolonged touch, off color or suggestive comments, and over-personal appreciation. For some of us, those interactions fill an unmet need. Without intending to, we encourage the behavior; after all it feels good to be noticed and appreciated. **If you struggle with insecurity, low self esteem, love-hunger, or appreciation-hunger, you would do well to deal with these issues. When those problems fester they leave you ripe for the inappropriate attention of other men.** Inappropriate attention grows easily to adultery.

If you answered yes to the question, "Do you think about other men who will be present when you dress?" I want to speak directly to you. If, as you prepare for your day, or a meeting, or an interaction you find yourself dressing for a man, be very careful!

Your mind has already crossed a boundary. This person has invaded your thought life, crowding out your exclusive relationship with your husband. Somewhere in your mind, you are interested in pleasing that man, garnering his attention, or his approval. These are dangerous precursors to establishing an inappropriate relationship.

If you find yourself in this position, do the things we have already mentioned. Tell a wise Christian friend about your temptation. Deliberately choose to avoid unnecessary contact with the man. When you must be with him, be certain that someone else is present and deliberately choose modest and appropriate clothing. Consider speaking with your husband about your temptation. Don't be afraid to share the reasons that this man's attention is so flattering. Ask your husband for support and prayer. Whatever you do, pay attention to the situation and take immediate action. As so many experts have pointed out, sexual sin does not occur spontaneously. It begins in our thoughts and grows slowly and insidiously outward. **Only with vigilant self-awareness can we avoid the temptations which occur when our sin nature collides with our culture's sexual values.**

CHAPTER 4

The Lies We Believe

Ours is a nutty world. On one hand, we display sexuality at every opportunity. On the other, we are afraid to speak of it in healthy ways. When I was a girl, my mother never spoke about sex. She only knew I'd started my menstrual cycle because I called her at work. I thought I'd entered some magic sorority, and I think I expected her to welcome me aboard; instead, she seemed completely unimpressed.

Looking back, she was probably embarrassed by my call. At the time, the new age of sex education had hardly begun. As part of our physical education program, Mrs. Quinn taught us in groups segregated by sex. As I remember there was no mention of birth control, and no encouragement to abstain until marriage. The curriculum was mostly about menstrual periods and pregnancy.

As a child, I watched situation comedy on a small black and white television where married couples slept in twin beds. On-screen kisses were timed so that they didn't last too long. In my early teens, women's liberation resulted in bra burning on city streets. Birth control pills and *Cosmopolitan* magazine convinced many women that unmarried sex was their right—just as important as equal pay for equal work. More than a right, these liberated women proposed that unmarried sex was the key to happiness, power, freedom and a full life.

From that explosive beginning, our sex-infused media has progressed to portraying sex acts on daytime television. Prime time programing regularly includes adultery and premarital sex. Homosexual characters and homosexual relationships are as ordinary as commercials. And frequently, as the media tries to push our "sensitivities," the homosexual character is the only calm, wise influence in an otherwise crazy cast.

We've been inundated; we are the frog placed in warm water, now boiled to death—without so much as a quiver of objection.

The problem is that along with this new openness toward our "natural" sexuality, we've been fed a great many lies. In the course of this chapter, we'll begin to confront the lies of our culture. As you read this week's lesson, keep your eyes open. If you are studying this book in a group, watch your favorite media outlets for other lies—both subtle and overt. Cut out ads, articles, pictures, and come to your next meeting prepared to share examples.

As a believer who trusts God's Word for direction, you know that God wants us to examine our thoughts, to compare what we see with God's standards. Look at this scripture:

> Don't copy the behavior and customs of this world, but let God transform you into a new person by changing the way you think. Then you will learn to know God's will for you, which is good and pleasing and perfect.
> ROMANS 12:2

Do you see it? In this Romans passage, we are encouraged to avoid falling in line with our culture's values. We are encouraged to consider our thought life, and to change it so that we conform ourselves instead to God's standards.

In order to do that, we must recognize the lies our world conveys. Pay attention not only to the lies themselves, but also to the ways those lies influence your sexual satisfaction. The world has a twisted view of God's plan. Don't let that view ruin your delight in the gift you share with your spouse.

Lie Number One: Only beautiful women win.

If I could wave a magic wand and wipe away any single weakness among women, it would be our tendency to compare ourselves with one another. The advertising media plays to this weakness, showing us endless pictures of the slimmest women, with perfect hair and make-up, dressed in designer clothing and jewelry. Most of these images have been digitally altered—skin smoothed, legs lengthened, hair tamed. In the end, we aren't even comparing ourselves to a real woman!

Even beautiful models experience constant pressure to compare themselves to others. Tyra Banks, host of *America's Next Top Model*, remembers a time in Milan when she was told she was too fat to work. It was a turning point in her life. Did she accept someone else's standard of beauty? Or did she accept her own?

All of us are tempted to compare. We wonder, is my body small enough? Is my skin clear enough, smooth enough? Do I wear the right clothes, the right make-up, the right accessories? Are my clothes in fashion? Is my hair the right texture, color and cut? These endless comparisons accompany us right into our bedroom. See if you've heard this lie whispered into your ear. . .

Only beautiful women have great sex lives.

This lie comes in endless variations. Do these sound familiar?

> Men only desire beautiful women.
> Ordinary looking women get the "left over" men.
> If I want to keep him, I have to look like her. . .

These kinds of lies have the ability to steal our confidence. Believing them, we focus only on our flaws, forgetting the great strengths and gifts that God has given us.

Unchecked, comparison leaves us dissatisfied with our body, reluctant to share it openly and joyfully with our spouse. It can force us to dress in the dark and wear flannel to bed. Taken to its full potential, this lie (that only beautiful women are desirable) can leave us filled with envy. We can harbor resentment toward whatever body type society deems the contemporary version of approved beauty. And, we can begin to resent the beautiful body God gave us.

Over the last fifty years, I've watched fickle fashion editors change their definition of beauty. We've gone from appreciating the curvy shapeliness of Marilyn Monroe to desiring the rail thin, asexual beauty of Twiggy. Since then, fashion has moved from its appreciation of "white only" models to its current preoccupation with African-American-Asian women.

The problem here is deeper than *who* defines beautiful. When we compare ourselves with others, and believe that only beautiful people get the best stuff (whether that be money, jobs, men, or even sex), we open ourselves to all kinds of obsessions that keep us from trusting God to provide for our needs. That same lie can keep us from appreciating everything God has given us.

Comparison not only opens the door to jealousy and ingratitude, it may also drive us to waste precious time, energy and resources trying to achieve whatever is today's measure of beauty. You see this urgent desperation in today's fascination with cosmetic surgery. You see it in young women having breast augmentation surgery before they graduate from high school. You see it in fad diets and liposuction. You see it in the massive growth of the beauty products industry. You see it in gym memberships, personal trainers and diet supplements—not that these in themselves are explicitly sinful. However, when discipline becomes an obsession, you can be certain that your attention and affection have been hijacked. When any woman chooses cosmetic procedures numbering in the hundreds, this lie has developed into a full blown compulsion.

But what is the truth? What does the Bible tell us?

First, the Bible declares that the design of our body is no accident. Read this passage excerpted from Psalm 139:

> You made all the delicate inner parts of my body and knit me together in my mother's womb. Thank you for making me so wonderfully complex! Your workmanship is marvelous—how well I know it. You watched me as I was formed in utter seclusion, as I was woven together in the dark of the womb. You saw me before I was born. . .
> PSALM 139:13–16

God designed you. Your skin. Your eyes. Your hair. Your body type. Your intelligence. Your gifts. Yes, even your nose. What scientists refer to as the genetic lottery is truly the loving design of your heavenly Father. Somehow, He put all those genes together in a way that pleases Him, allowing them unique expression that will bring Him ultimate glory.

When we allow dissatisfaction to fester in our self-image, we not only undermine our sexuality, we also express our disapproval of God's custom design. Who are you to doubt God's workmanship? Didn't He know what He was doing when He created you?

The lie that only beautiful people experience success, live happy lives, and enjoy good husbands will either trap us in a cycle of striving or it will leave us with a constant sense of discontent—in our work, our calling, our purpose, and yes, even in our sexual expression with our husband! At its root, the lie doubts

God's sovereignty. It believes that beauty— not God—is in charge. The lie believes that God cannot or will not bless us outside of someone else's definition of perfect physical beauty.

I am no different than most women. I have struggled with this issue. Let me give you a personal example:

You can't tell from my promotional pictures, but the truth is that I have the legs of a football player—shaped roughly like the pillars found on the porch of a southern antebellum mansion. I come by them genetically, and I've given them to all my children. During World War I, when my great-grandfather joined the army, his spats had to be custom made to fit his enormous calves. As a child, my father used to speak to his friends about me saying, "Look at those calves. If I thought it'd do any good I'd wrap her legs in rubber and make her run around the block."

In my father's words, I heard rejection and disapproval. I grew up resenting my strong, muscular legs. Even now, I sometimes feel a twinge of regret when I see a beautiful woman with slim beautiful calves. Imagine my surprise when my husband expresses delight in what he calls my very "shapely legs." I have believed the lie for so long that even now, so many years later, I am still surprised by his expressions of appreciation. How many years have I wasted wishing I had someone else's legs? How often have I tried to hide them, because they don't fit some preconceived notion of beautiful, when in fact, they please my husband very much?

Paul warns us about the danger of comparison in the book of Romans. Here is the passage:

> Because of the privilege and authority God has given me, I give each of you this warning: Don't think you are better than you really are. Be honest in your evaluation of yourselves, measuring yourselves by the faith God has given us.
> ROMANS 12: 3

Time for Reflection

Think about the ways you have compared yourself to other women. List the ways you believe you come up short. For instance:
- My body is too curvy.
- I wear glasses.
- I'm not as smart as. . .

Comparison can also lead to pride. Do you have prideful thoughts comparing yourself to others? What are they?

What about "sound thoughts," or realistic assessments of your strengths? Can you honestly list some of your strengths below?

How has the current definition of beauty affected your ability to accept your body? Are you unsatisfied? How?

What do you think are your best physical assets?

Be honest. Has your husband expressed appreciation for any part of your body? Which? Do you listen to him? Or, do you mentally negate what he says? What would happen if you said simply, "Thank you."

Different but Confident

The Bible talks about a woman whose beauty didn't fit the standards of her day. Though she was aware of her differences, she did not let them keep her from enjoying the pleasure of her sexuality. Here is the passage:

> I am dark but beautiful,
> O women of Jerusalem—
> dark as the tents of Kedar,
> dark as the curtains of Solomon's tents.
>
> Don't stare at me because I am dark—
> the sun has darkened my skin.
> My brothers were angry with me;
> they forced me to care for their vineyards,
> so I couldn't care for myself—my own vineyard.
> SONG OF SOLOMON 1:5–6

The bride in the Song of Solomon felt the disapproval of the women of Jerusalem. Though she was not fair skinned, she did not refrain from enjoying her husband. Did her dark skin keep him from enjoying her? Look at what the bridegroom says:

> You are beautiful, my darling, beautiful beyond words. Your eyes are like doves behind your veil.
> Your hair falls in waves, like a flock of goats winding down the slopes of Gilead. Your teeth are as white as sheep, recently shorn and freshly washed.
> Your smile is flawless, each tooth matched with its twin.
> Your lips are like scarlet ribbon; your mouth is inviting.
> SONG OF SONGS 4:1–3

Lie Number Two: Great sex just happens.

Sometimes, what we don't know *can* hurt us. If everything you knew about sex, you learned from the media, you would find yourself in a desert, devoid of information and lacking in godly wisdom. Think about situation comedy. Here, producers teach that good sex between a man and a woman is nothing more than finding the right key for your particular lock. You must simply keep looking until you find the perfect key.

If you listen to the media, you might believe that great sex just happens. Never, in any depiction of sex, do audiences observe couples doing the loving work required to improve their sex lives. Couples don't talk about what is bothering them. They make no requests of one another. They don't experience the disappointments of being human. They don't forgive one another for those human disappointments. This is because one of the lies is that great sex just happens. And of course, the whole thing is more entertaining, more sad, or tragic, or funny when it doesn't.

In truth, healthy sex in a loving marriage takes time, commitment and effort. In the beginning, the design gap between men and women can cause a great deal of frustration. Men, who generally come with an "instant boil" setting, have trouble functioning with the "slow simmer" design of women. Real couples take time to figure out how they will handle those differences.

As people change, as over the course of a lifetime individuals will (both physically and emotionally), the sexual relationship between them must change as well. Couples grow older, they experience hormonal and emotional changes, their bodies age, their joints lose flexibility. Occasionally an accident or serious illness will rob one partner of pleasure. What once pleased may now hurt. What once was enough, may now be too much. Learning.

Growing. Adjusting. This, not switching partners, makes for great sex between a man and his wife.

Lie Number Three: My spiritual obligation is to submit to sex, whether or not I enjoy it.

This lie actually has two parts. The first is that sex is not meant for my enjoyment. This is almost as destructive as the lie that great sex just happens. I'll cover the second aspect—that I should submit to my husband's every sexual whim—in lie number four.

Though I did not know my maternal grandmother well, the family rumor is that she was constantly angry because my grandfather wanted to enjoy an active sexual relationship with her. As a practicing Catholic her access to birth control was restricted to the rhythm method. Whether her anger was really about sex, or perhaps about feeling forced into giving birth to such a large family, no one can say. Whatever the reason, the result was a simmering resentment that, family rumor has it, poisoned the relationship between my grandparents and changed the atmosphere of their home. What a tragedy!

What does the Bible say? Consider the words of the young bride in the Song of Solomon:

> Oh feed me with your love—your raisins and your apples—
> for I am utterly lovesick! His left hand is under my head
> and his right hand embraces me. (2:5,6)
>
> One night, as I lay in bed, I yearned for my lover. (3:1)
>
> Awake, north wind! Rise up, south wind!
> Blow on my garden and spread its fragrance all around.
> Come into your garden, my love;
> taste its finest fruits. (4:16)

(Bride speaking of her lover) None can rival him. His mouth is sweetness itself; he is desirable in every way. Such, O women of Jerusalem, is my lover, my friend. (5:16)

Clearly, this woman enjoyed her sexual relationship with Solomon. She looked forward to being together sexually, and missed him when he was away. She dreamed about him during his long absences. In fact, if you read the entire text, the bride's sexual enjoyment of the King became part of his own sexual pleasure.

Dr. Kevin Leman in his book *Sheet Music*, says this about a woman's sexual pleasure. **"Most men get much more sexual pleasure out of watching their wife reach orgasm than they do experiencing their own. A man's orgasm usually pales in comparison to that experienced by his wife."**

If Dr. Leman is correct—that men love to have their wives enjoy their sexuality—it may be the most well-kept secret in the sexual universe!

Let's correct the lie. If sex is a gift from God, designed for pleasure, to deeply bond husband and wife together, to protect the family, to uniquely express the love that a man and woman share, then why wouldn't it be your spiritual obligation to enjoy, not just tolerate, the gift? Did God create the gift just for males? If that were so, why involve women at all?

And if scripture approves of a woman's enjoyment of her husband (as it clearly does), then shouldn't you make it your goal to enjoy your sexual relationship with your husband as much as is physically possible for you?

Absolutely.

Statistically, not every woman achieves orgasm with every sexual encounter. (You are not the only one out there who sometimes struggles to achieve orgasm) However, statistics should not limit your hopes. Reaching orgasm is a learned skill. You can learn this physical skill in the same way you learn to play a cello, to waterski, to run on a treadmill, or to knit. It's possible for you to achieve an orgasm that (to use Dr. Lehman's words) drops your husband's jaw. Doing so will certainly please you; it will absolutely delight your husband.

If you are a young woman, perhaps recently married, you may not yet have experienced the sexual gratification that is yours. I assure you, the future can be different. Let your husband know that you really want to figure out how to enjoy sex as much as he does. Ask for his help in accomplishing this goal. I think you'll have a very willing assistant. Try reading Dr. Leman's book together. Try his methods. Read other books by reliable Christian authors and gather more information.

When our children were very young, my husband and I spent Sunday afternoons (as the children napped), reading a book about sex. We read it together and then practiced what we learned. Thirty years is a long time to remember what happened on any particular Sunday afternoon. But I remember those weeks fondly.

Make enjoying sex your goal. Practice with your spouse. Talk about and compare your various approaches. Evaluate. Change. Try again. Most importantly, plan on lots of physical "warm up," activities. A woman's sex-engine needs time to get up to speed. If you depend on lots of kissing and caressing, be sure to let your spouse know. As you practice, take sex slowly, give your husband lots of verbal feedback, and see what happens!

We'll talk about these ideas more thoroughly in the chapter about growing your sexual enjoyment. For now, please consider this critically important truth: **God meant for you to enjoy your sexual relationship.** That enjoyment can be learned, just as any physical activity. Don't give in to the lie that you should submit rather than enjoy!

If, for some reason, you find yourself stuck, don't give up. Perhaps you need professional help. For some, vaginal pain or muscular tightness (called Vaginismus), can prevent true relaxation and pleasure. In this condition severe pain accompanies the insertion of the penis, or tampons, or even a pelvic exam. Trust me, this kind of pain isn't normal, and it can be helped tremendously by proper therapies.

There are physicians and physical therapists whose extensive training and sex-specific expertise can work wonders with even the most difficult cases. Consult your primary care doctor for a referral and then do whatever it takes to follow through.

Sometimes, hormone changes leave the vagina extremely dry, causing pain with intercourse. This too can be helped by various hormone therapies both local (applied to the vagina itself) and systemic.

In some cases, pain during intercourse can signal serious disease—especially when such pain is a change in the normal course of events or accompanied by other symptoms. Be sure to check with your doctor should this happen.

Learning to enjoy your sex life could just change your marriage. As you practice, don't forget. **Sex between a husband and wife is about relationship—not baby making, and not orgasm. Don't let these important goals distract you from the loving relationship you share.** Don't let expectations (individual or mutual) and disappointments come between the two of you. Your relationship is too valuable for that.

Time for Reflection

Thinking about your sex-life: Is there one thing you wish your husband "got" about how your body functions? Are there things about your sexual relationship that you would change if you could?

Have you ever successfully discussed your sex life together? What happened? Why do you think that worked?

Do you ever find yourself feeling resentful about love-making? What are you resentful about? Have you talked to your husband about the way you felt? What action might you take to mitigate resentment.

Do you ever feel embarrassed to ask for what pleases you?

Have you ever felt embarrassed during intimate time with your husband? Where might that emotion have come from?

If you could have sex proceed in EXACTLY the perfect way, what would that look like? Have you ever shared this dream with your husband?

Lie Number Four: Women should just submit.

In a variation of the no enjoyment lie, believers sometimes emphasize the "submit" aspect of the sexual relationship between a man and a woman. Believing that she should submit to her husband's every sexual whim, some women end up feeling resentful—not to mention humiliated, manipulated, or exhausted.

Like most lies, this one comes wrapped in partial truth. Let's look at the passage which gave birth to the lie. You can read it here:

> Now regarding the questions you asked in your letter. Yes, it is good to abstain from sexual relations. But because there is so much sexual immorality, each man should have his own wife, and each woman should have her own husband. The husband should fulfill his wife's sexual needs, and the wife should fulfill her husband's needs. The wife gives authority over her body to her husband, and the husband gives authority over his body to his wife. Do not deprive each other of sexual relations, unless you both agree to refrain from sexual intimacy for a limited time so you can give yourselves more completely to prayer. Afterward, you should come together again so that Satan won't be able to tempt you because of your lack of self-control.
>
> 1 CORINTHIANS 7:1–5

In the hands of a demanding husband, this passage could be used to support the lie. "You don't have to like it. I don't even *care* if you like it. You just have to do it. That's what the Bible says." After all, the passage does instruct a woman to fulfill her husband's sexual needs. Right?

But that is an incomplete and therefore inaccurate reading. Look carefully; before Paul commands us not to deny one another, he instructs a man to fulfill his wife's sexual needs. This makes it clear that women do indeed have sexual needs. The woman's needs may be, and most certainly are, different than those of her husband. She may require a more tender, more cautious, more considerate sexual approach, but she needs the approach!

While a wife should do her best to care for her husband, she should do so *while at the same time,* **helping him to meet her own needs.** In that way, she helps him to fulfill this important scriptural mandate. The scripture clearly emphasizes a mutual concern for one another.

Of course, no husband can meet his wife's sexual needs if she doesn't help him understand what those needs are. Young women may not even recognize their own needs. With time your needs will become apparent. Your scriptural obligation is to share them, gently and thoughtfully, with your husband.

Perhaps you need to spend more time touching and being touched, rather than rushing into the "main event." Perhaps you need to spend time cuddling after having sex. Perhaps, like me, you simply can't wake up at two AM and respond to your husband's sexual needs. (I am absolutely not able to sleep after sex! I could go running though.) In our case my need for sleep trumped all desire for middle of the night sexual activity. We've managed to survive without it!

By taking the time to talk about these things, preferably in the bright light of day, when you both are feeling good about your relationship, you can make your needs known. Then, applying the Corinthians passage to your sexual relationship with your husband, you can affirm this truth: You are both responsible for meeting one another's sexual needs.

It is only in the atmosphere of mutual care, mutual submission, and mutual consideration that the sexual relationship between a husband and wife reaches its highest potential. When both partners are having their sexual needs met, both partners are far less likely to feel justified in looking elsewhere for sexual fulfillment. Meeting one another's needs does, as Paul says, protect both husband and wife from Satan's temptations.

Time for Reflection

When you think about your own sexuality, what needs do you think are important for your husband to meet?

As you think about your relationship with your husband, what needs has he expressed to you? What needs have you observed? How are you doing at meeting his needs?

Do the answers to these questions give you ideas for discussion with your husband? Write them here:

As we think about sexual enjoyment and the concept of orgasm, it's time to reflect on your own experience. Do you have trouble experiencing orgasm during intercourse?

Is that frustrating for you? For your husband? How does that frustration manifest itself?

Have you talked about this with your husband? (remember how few of the women in my class were comfortable talking about sex? Here is where it really counts!) Have you done any reading or studying about the issue? Have you worked at it together?

Are you experiencing shame because of this issue? Does it make you or your spouse want to avoid sex?

Have you talked about it with your physician? Did he offer suggestions? Have you asked for outside help? Would you consider outside help?

Lie Number Five: If my husband sins sexually, it's my fault.

There are so many lies about sexuality floating around in our culture. This one has many unhealthy implications. Somehow, this lie implies, because of my failure he had to look elsewhere for sexual fulfillment. You'll see this lie expressed by Christians (who ought to know better) in chapter ten.

When it comes to sin, God doesn't hand out free passes. Sexual sin is no exception. Look at the Corinthian passage below:

> . . . Don't you realize that your bodies are actually parts of Christ? Should a man take his body, which is part of Christ, and join it to a prostitute? Never! And don't you realize that if a man joins himself to a prostitute, he becomes one body with her? For the Scriptures say, "The two are united into one." But the person who is joined to the Lord is one spirit with him.
>
> Run from sexual sin! No other sin so clearly affects the body as this one does. For sexual immorality is a sin against your own body. Don't you realize that your body is the temple of the Holy Spirit, who lives in you and was given to you by God? You do not belong to yourself, for God bought you with a high price. So you must honor God with your body.
> 1 CORINTHIANS 6:15–20

Please note that in verse 18, Paul doesn't say, "Run from sexual sin, unless of course, you are unfulfilled at home, in which case we all understand." Paul's admonition comes without equivocation. Run! That's his command, plain and simple.

As I bring a different perspective to this lie, be ready to stretch your thinking. My arguments are not direct. This lie is not directly confronted in scripture. Instead, follow along with me as I look back to the very first sin ever described in the Bible. You'll find it in Genesis 3. In this passage, Eve is in the garden with the serpent who challenges her understanding of God's restriction.

Can she eat the fruit of the tree in the center of the garden?

At that critical moment, Eve looks again at the fruit. It looked delicious; she believed Satan's lies—that the fruit had the power to make her as wise as God. She buys the lie, bites the apple, and suffers the consequences.

When God confronts the man and the woman (Genesis 3:11–13), you will discover the most ingenious although brief example of blame-shifting ever recorded. Here is the conversation:

> And He said, "Who told you that you were naked? Have you eaten from the tree of which I commanded you that you should not eat?"
>
> Then the man said, "The woman whom You gave to be with me, she gave me of the tree, and I ate."
>
> And the Lord God said to the woman, "What is this you have done?"
>
> The woman said, "The serpent deceived me, and I ate."

When God confronts the man, he blames the woman. When God confronts the woman, she blames the serpent. No human in the entire story takes responsibility for their own actions. Not one.

Things haven't changed much when it comes to adultery. Society has blamed the wife for a husband's adultery for so long that women have begun to believe the lie. It's a little bit like blaming the bank who has been robbed for having had money in the first place. Or blaming poverty for the robber's poor choices.

Did you realize that even perfect partners experience betrayal? In fact God, who is perfect in every way, had trouble maintaining a faithful relationship with his people. Consider his anguish expressed in these excerpts from Jeremiah 2, beginning in verse 2:

> This is what the LORD says: I remember how eager you were to please me as a young bride long ago, how you loved me and followed me even through the barren wilderness. . . This is what the LORD says: What sin did your ancestors find in me that led them to stay so far?
>
> (God speaking, verse 13) For my people have done two evil things. They have forsaken me—the fountain of living water. And they have dug for themselves cracked cisterns that can hold no water at all.
>
> (verse 31) Oh my people, listen to the words of the LORD! Have I been like a desert to Israel? Have I been to them a land of darkness? ... how you plot and scheme to win your lovers. The most experienced prostitute could learn from you!

Unfaithfulness happened—even to a perfect God.

Why? Though I'm no scholar, it seems to me that the scripture shows us that our sin nature pulls us strongly in a downward direction. If Israel, who lived in a barren land, could abandon the fresh water bubbling up from a living God, choosing instead to seek a dry cracked well, then I believe the evidence is clear: **The pull to abandon the safe, the good, the loving is very strong. While that excuses no one, it may help to explain what happens when a husband or wife betrays their loving spouse.**

How can we blame a husband's unfaithfulness on his perfectly imperfect wife? We can't. We all know dozens of perfectly imperfect women who enjoy faithful husbands. Blame shifting never accomplished anything. Not in the Garden of Eden. Not in your marriage.

When adultery occurs, there are often pre-existing issues in the marriage. Every marriage has issues. Every relationship has difficulty; no amount of difficulty, large or small, gives your partner permission to betray the promises made on your wedding day!

It would not be fair to leave this lie without exposing its corollary. If it is true that women cannot be blamed for their husband's infidelity, it is also true that men cannot be blamed when their wives begin affairs (either emotional or physical) with other men.

I have cried with women who were already involved, or who were considering involvement with men other than their spouses. These women tend to blame their husbands. "He doesn't care about me. He never talks to me. We don't have anything in common any more. I'm so lonely."

While these problems are absolutely real (and I recognize the deep pain these women experience), we cannot allow pain to make our choices for us. Our exclusive relationship with our spouse demands that we make whatever changes are necessary to keep and or restore strong emotional bonds with our spouse.

You might be surprised to hear me say that it is possible that women sometimes expect too much of their emotional ties with their husbands. (Not every marriage lie comes from the secular media). This commonly held expectation may arrise from the following popular Christian lie:

Lie Number Six: My husband must be my best friend.

While it is rarely stated with such clarity, I hear this implied all the time, especially from Christian speakers, teachers and pastors. You've heard it too. The guest speaker introduces his spouse as his "best friend." While I cannot evaluate the truth of their personal experience, I find myself doubting the subtle message they transmit. When speakers tell audiences that they are "married to my best friend," they suggest that this should be the norm, or worse, that the Bible requires this of all marriages. Nothing could be further from the truth.

In fact, I wonder if the lie actually deepens the sense of loneliness and dissatisfaction that many women feel. Why? Because women may unconsciously shift enormous and unfair expectations onto their husbands, anticipating behavior these men were not created for. The idea sells books, but is it Biblically reliable?

Truth? Men and women have very different kinds of friendships. Men spend time together "doing," (golf, fishing, hiking, boating) while women tend to spend time "being," (coffee, visiting, etc). Even when women do activities together, those activities are far more about interaction than accomplishment. Women tend to process feelings, while men tend to accomplish goals or solve problems. This is not to say that men have no feelings. They do.

What I am saying is that this lie might lead a lonely woman (experiencing estrangement and dissatisfaction with her husband's inabilbity to meet her needs), to justify (to herself and others) an inappropriate relationship with another man. That justification might lead to infidelity. Instead, every woman would do well to ask herself some serious questions, like the ones which follow;

Time for Reflection

Do you experience loneliness in your marriage relationship? To what do you attribute this feeling?

What does the term "best friend" mean to you? Be honest. Have you expected your husband to be your best friend? Why?

How is he doing in that role? Does he fail? Occasionally? Often? Never?

Can you think of a single scripture, or example where husbands and wives are **commanded** to be "best" friends?

List the qualities of a friend. Then check off the qualities that your husband exibits toward you.

Make no mistake, all of the "one another" commands of the New Testament should be clearly displayed in our relationship with our believing spouse. After all, in the Christian marriage, husbands and wives are not only spouses but they are also brothers and sisters in Christ. (There are more than 61 one another commands, including "pray for one another, forgive one another, encourage one another, and many many more). Look up the term "one another" in your concordance. List the one "one another" command that you find hardest to exhibit toward your spouse:

Do you have many women-friends? Do you make time to cultivate those relationships? How might you do this better?

Do you think it is reasonable to expect any ONE person to be your best friend? Does "best friend" mean "only" friend to you? Where did you get this concept? Is it fair to the other person?

What happens if you have only one "best" friend, and that friend is taken away? Have you experienced this? What happened as a result? How might the concept of best friend be unwise?

Easing Your Expectaions
Is it possible that by easing up on the unfair expectations you place on your husband, you free him to be what God made him to be? Might doing this might create more time for him to interact with other Godly men? As you ease your expectations you might discover that he has more desire for talking, sharing, and interaction with you.

I find it interesting that these lies are intricately related. By believing one (that my husband should be my best friend), we accept another (it is his fault that I was unfaithful). In the end, we find ourselves betraying our most precious relationship. Eventually, we are caught in the snare of infidelity. Don't let that happen!

Watch Joseph face sexual temptation in the Old Testament.

> Now Joseph was a very handsome and well-built young man. And about this time, Potiphar's wife began to desire him and invited him to sleep with her. But Joseph refused. "Look," he told her, 'my master trusts me with everything in his entire household. . . How could I ever do such a wicked thing? It would be a great sin against God."
> GENESIS 39: 6–9

Isn't it intersting that as Joseph acknowledges his debt to Potiphar, Joseph is most worried about offending God? Think of all the excuses Joeseph had. After all, he was lonely. He was deserted in a foreign country. He was without accountability. Who would ever know? Certainly Potiphar's wife would never tell. His sexual needs were not being met (a real drive in a very young man, as Joseph was). Still, Joseph refused to sin.

His primary motivation for sexual purity was his deep commitment to God. He would not fail God in this way. I find this story of resistance inspiring.

Is there healing after infidelity? There can be. You will read three stories about infidelity in chapter ten. However I would be so bold as to say that healing after an affair begins only when a man or a woman takes full responsibility for his or her own sin. When a man (for example) can say, "I did it. It was my decision. I knew better, and I did it anyway," he has taken the first step toward reconciliation with God.

When he takes responsibility for the ways his actions have wounded his spouse, he has begun the journey toward reconciliation with his wife. That road, a long and difficult journey, can lead to a stronger marriage, but it takes hard work, many tears and deep introspection from both partners.

I have seen marriages survive infidelity. In every one of those cases, the offending partner did the work to prove he had changed. He or she took the time to earn back the spouse's trust. It was never easy, never instantaneous. But when the work is done, God is glorified.

If you discover your spouse has been unfaithful, begin by getting support for yourself. Try not to take immediate action or make critical decisions. Those first days after discovery are very important in determining the course of your relationship.

Time for Reflection

In this chapter we've looked at several cultural lies. There are others. I've listed a few below. If you are studying with a group, discuss these together. Try to identify their origin. Ask yourself how they are perpetuated. Think about how they might affect married couples. If you can think of other lies, list them as well:

- My private, personal sin has no effect on others.
- A sinful sexual relationship between two consenting adults won't hurt anyone.

- When couples fight all the time, divorce is best for everyone involved (especially for the children).
- All good sex is hot, passionate, sweaty and looks like it does in the movies.
- Divorce leaves no lasting scars on individuals.

I hope you haven't been discouraged by this long and intense chapter. A wise woman questions the deeply held beliefs of both her church and her culture.

I hope that instead of "going with the flow," you have learned to compare what you hear to the truth of scripture. I hope that you've learned to think of your husband differently, to let go of unreasonable expectations and to appreciate him more deeply.

This week, I want you to conduct an experiement:

Considering your family's schedule and your own obligations, plan a sexual encounter for your spouse. Put some effort into planning the event. Include activities your husband will especially enjoy. Then, when you have the event in mind, write out an invitation for your husband. Make it clear that you have his sexual pleasure in mind. Give it to him early enough in the day that he has time to anticipate your invitation. Put the kids to bed early, or take advantage of a time when they are away.

After your date, reflect on what happened. How did he react? Was he pleased? Surprised? Was he able to express his appreciation? How did *you* feel about doing this activity? Pay attention to those feelings. Write down your reflections below. If you are studying with a group, be prepared to share these observations. You will benefit from discussing how planning and inviting influenced your thinking about sex, your thinking about your husband, and about your own role in your sexual relationship.

CHAPTER 5

Sex and the Difficult Marriage

Years ago, when my oldest daughter was first engaged, her fiancé asked me this question. "Bette, do you believe that God has one right person in mind for each individual to marry?" I admit it; his question gave me pause. I didn't want to mess with Jeff's theology.

Here was my answer. "Your question implies that God's plan for marriage is that each partner be deliriously happy all the days of his life. It implies that if you could just find God's right person for you, your troubles would be over. I don't think that's what God has in mind. It doesn't mesh with the rest of scripture."

"The plan," I said, "is far more about you **becoming** the right person **for your spouse**, than it is that you find the right person to marry."

That answer left my normally chatty son-in-law quite speechless. I'd managed to give him a far more profound issue to ponder. In my view, scripture tells us God is far more interested in transformation than comfort. Our best questions might be, "Can I become the spouse my husband deserves? Am I willing?"

Doing this demands that we mature in Christ. It demands action without consideration of reward or payback. This isn't the easy way; it certainly isn't the way of the world. However, it is the way of Christ.

> It's like this: When I was a child, I spoke and thought and reasoned as a child. But when I grew up, I put away childish things.
> I CORINTHIANS 13:11

> For you have been called to live in freedom, my brothers and sisters. But don't use your freedom to satisfy your sinful nature. Instead, use your freedom to serve one another in love.
> GALATIONS 5: 13

For the purposes of this chapter, I will define "bad sex," as any pattern of sexual behavior that is dissatisfying to either partner. At the risk of oversimplifying, for many men the issue is nothing more than not enough sex. For many women, the issue is more about the quality of her sexual interaction with her husband.

A difficult marriage is one where the couple experiences persistent, unresolved conflict which is significant enough to one or both of the partners that it colors that partner's satisfaction with the union. This conflict can have its root in something as simple as child rearing, or as complex as addiction or abuse.

In the course of this chapter, we can't begin to cover all the issues facing a difficult marriage. Neither can we discuss all the problems involved in what some call "bad sex." But hopefully, by understanding the importance of these issues, you will find the courage to change. Only you can discover and use the tools that will modify your responses and belief systems. However, the results are well worth it. Healing is absolutely possible.

We will discuss the connections between a couple's sexual relationship and the health of their marriage. No matter how much we wish to disconnect the two concepts, in truth, sexual satisfaction and marital satisfaction are deeply interrelated.

The only way to avoid persistent conflict and the sexual dissatisfaction that arises from it, is to begin to look at our conflict resolution patterns, which we will explore in the following reflection. Think about how you and your husband solve problems. Do you follow scriptural advice?

Time for Reflection

On your wedding day, how much conflict did you anticipate you and your spouse would experience in marriage?

Does reality match those expectations?

In a few words, describe the pattern of your disagreements.

Is there a persistent winner in your disagreements?

Do you truly solve problems, or do problems become shelved, only to arise in another context? Can you think of an example?

If you could change one thing about the pattern of your conflict resolution (as a couple), what would it be?

Using this passage answer the following questions:

> "If another believer sins against you, go privately and point out the offense. If the other person listens and confesses it, you have won that person back. But if you are unsuccessful, take one or two others with you and go back again, so that everything you say may be confirmed by two or three witnesses. If the person still refuses to listen, take your case to the church. Then if he or she won't accept the church's decision, treat that person as a pagan or a corrupt tax collector."
>
> MATTHEW 18: 15–17

The context of this passage describes conflict resolution in the body of Christ. Clearly, in a marriage, a husband and wife cannot let most offenses cause permanent seperation. However, this passage gives us a godly pattern for resolving conflict. What is the first step? Is this what you do?

Should your spouse refuse to listen, what might be the second step? In your case, who might the "other" be?

Think about the role of the marriage counselor in the context of this passage. What part might a marriage counselor play in this advice (whether or not you choose to consult with a counselor)?

Read the following passage:

> Don't use foul or abusive language. Let everything you say be good and helpful, so that your words will be an encouragement to those who hear them.And do not bring sorrow to God's Holy Spirit by the way you live. Remember, he has identified you as his own, guaranteeing that you will be saved on the day of redemption. Get rid of all bitterness, rage, anger, harsh words, and slander, as well as all types of evil behavior. Instead, be kind to each other, tenderhearted, forgiving one another, just as God through Christ has forgiven you.
>
> EPHESIANS 4:29–32

These passages provide much counsel for married couples struggling with conflict. Make a list of the advice Paul gives regarding how to speak to your spouse.

Are you following Paul's advice? What is your biggest struggle in this area? What **one thing** might you do to bring change?

Sex Counts—Especially When Things are Difficult

Every marriage experiences it to some degree. Conflict is a normal part of two people living together for a lifetime. Perhaps it happens when one partner begins a new job. Or conflict arises when she decides to return to college and finish her degree. We struggled through our children's very early years. The constant demands of a new business, coupled with four young children was, for us, nearly too much to handle.

In our area, (near Joint Base Lewis McChord), many couples struggle with long deployments to the Middle East. Some of these couples face multiple deployments, with husbands gone for months at a time, year after year. When they are reunited many military couples experience the added trauma of combat related post-traumatic-stress. The couples in our military community are under tremendous pressure.

As tension mounts between a husband and his wife, the sexual relationship can begin to suffer. It is very rare for a man and woman to maintain a healthy sexual relationship in the midst of constant conflict and wounded feelings. In fact, for most couples marital tension degrades the sexual relationship. Though it seems improbable, some couples in the midst of stress can go for years without sexual contact. This is especially true of couples facing persistent difficulty in solving major marital issues.

What began as a small frustration can actually grow into a virtual Berlin Wall—keeping both partners isolated. In this case, the original wounds can pale in comparison to the deep chasms caused by a long period without sex.

It isn't hard to imagine. Isolation certainly hinders reconciliation. How can anyone safely scale the thick wall separating you from your spouse? It isn't easy. Interestingly though, the wall is actually made higher and more impenetrable—in fact fortified— when we allow marital discord to destroy our sexual intimacy. Let me tell you why.

Oxytocin and Bonding
Part of the secret may lie in the hormone oxytocin. Women who have experienced childbirth know this hormone intimately. It is responsible for the uterine contractions of labor. It is produced in large amounts after labor's second stage, stimulated by the distention of the cervix and vagina as the baby passes through the birth canal. It is responsible for the production of milk after the birth of a child. It is the hormone responsible for the "let down" reflex of nursing mothers. Researchers believe that this hormone is also responsible for the emotional bonding that occurs between a mother and her infant during early breastfeeding.

Somehow, as oxytocin bathes receptors in the brain, it creates a calming, emotional connectedness between mother and child. That calming relaxation may also cause many women to fall asleep immediately after nursing—though of course, pure undefiled exhaustion may have something to do with it. Who's to say?

While oxytocin plays an integral role in childbirth and nursing, the hormone has another side. **Oxytocin is released in both males and females during and after sexual intimacy. In males, this is the only time the male brain experiences an oxytocin "bath."** Scientists believe that the hormone may have two sexual functions. Most certainly it assists with the muscular contractions that promote the motility of sperm (and thus the fertilization of the female egg). It also has a profound effect on the male brain.

Oxytocin Helps Men Bond
Women experience this same bonding during sex. However, because women experience oxytocin in other ways, this smaller dose may not have as much significance as it does in males.

Why does this matter? Why should women pay attention to the connection between male bonding and and the oxytocin bath released by sex? **Because in most men, much emotional bonding happens because of sex. For most women, sex happens because of bonding.**

This difference highlights one of the many ways that men and women are different. The bonding that happens during that relaxed stage following sexual intercourse is responsible for the commonly used phrase, "pillow talk." It means that during the afterglow of sex, many couples find it easier to express themselves.

Does it matter?
When couples experience difficulty in their relationship, most women respond by pulling back from sexual intimacy. Remember, women tend to use sex as an expression of bondedness. For women, sex is a way to express their love, their connection and appreciation of their spouse. When things are working—when women feel cherished, valued, listened to, and loved—they are more likely to want sex. In fact, for most women, their willingness to initiate sex may be directly correlated with the strength of their positive feelings toward their husbands.

When they don't feel loved, few women are willing to engage in sex, let alone initiate.

On the other hand, men operate very differently. When they are denied sexual connection involving climax and ejaculation, men often feel themselves growing distant, even detached from their wives. If you add relational tension to infrequent sexual expression, most husbands really struggle to find their way back into a balanced relationship with their wives.

Time for Reflection

After you make love with your husband, what do you observe about his behavior? Does he draw closer?

After sex, how do you feel toward your spouse? Do you wish you could cuddle more? Talk? Touch? Does he?

Do you frequently enjoy the "afterglow" of your sexual relationship? Is there a way you might prolong that "glow?"

A Personal Example
While this oxytocin/bonding relationship is well-documented among therapists, I am familiar with this concept in a more personal way.

About twenty years ago, my husband and I experienced a difficult season in our marriage; it was both long lasting and excruciatingly difficult. After almost twenty years, we'd hit a wall. I was miserable. But I was also suffering physically. I'd begun having regular ovarian cysts which managed to completely disrupt my hormonal balance. I was struggling with depression and utter exhaustion.

To be fair, my husband worked far too many hours, and was neither emotionally nor physically available to our family. We had stopped investing in our relationship. I wasn't the only one who felt the strain. Not long ago, one of my children said to me, "I don't remember Dad being home when I was a child. In my mind you raised us."

That season was very difficult. Our children were wounded by our distress; though they are all doing well in their relationships and careers, they carry those wounds to this day. By God's pure and unadulterated grace our marriage was saved. Today we experience a very different kind of relationship.

It was during that season that I first learned this lesson about bondedness. Deeply wounded, I pulled back sexually. My husband felt disconnected and had difficulty finding the motivation to work on our relationship. We were the classic case of "she pulls back, he feels detached."

When a man is disconnected, it is much harder for him to work on the issues and difficulties of the relationship. It is his connectedness that motivates him to continue to try and improve his relationship with his wife. For him, sex is one of the most potent ways to build connectedness.

For this reason, even in times of stress and frustration, I suggest that both husband and wife prioritize the importance of their sexual relationship. I know that in some situations this may seem nearly impossible. However, if you can do it, you may give your husband the very motivation he needs to work on improving your relationship.

In some very difficult cases—like infidelity, pornography, or physical abuse, etc—your marriage counselor may suggest that you abstain from sex for a season. This works best if both partners are aware of and commit to this course of action. Certainly, you should follow your therapist's professional advice. However, remember the chemical/emotional reasons for resuming relations as soon as your therapist deems it both safe and wise.

When your marriage faces these very difficult issues, resuming sexual relations may be extremely difficult. If you find yourself unable to participate, consider getting help. You may need guidance to find the strength to forgive, or to move on. Don't be ashamed to ask for help. When it comes to leaving the past in the past, God knows that forgiveness is the only way. He can help you through it, I promise.

As you resume relations, build slowly. Begin as you would when you were dating. Hold hands. Kiss lightly. Touch gently. Spend time in deep kissing without the intention of intercourse. Give yourself the days or weeks you need to work yourself back into the place you were when your relationship was healthy.

I advise women to be very careful about using sex as punishment for bad behavior, or conversely, as a reward for good behavior. Sex is not a bargaining chip. Neither is it a training treat. Your spouse is not your dog.

A woman is a fool who chooses to use this holy intimacy selfishly. Doing so she unwittingly cuts herself off from the very connectedness and tenderness that she most desires in her relationship. When a woman uses sex as a manipulative tool, the act is no longer an expression of love. My advice: Don't use sexual power plays as a way to get your needs met.

When Discord Takes Over Your Marriage
When you and your husband face a marital crisis, the first temptation is to bury it. After all, most of your Christian friends seem to be doing just fine. Maybe if you just pray harder, read the Bible more, or get your "act together," eventually everything will turn itself around. Right?

This approach may work to solve a simple disagreement—choosing a new car, deciding which house to buy, etc. But when the crisis is longstanding, rarely will burying it work. Most of us find ourselves in marital crisis because of our own blind spots. We have weaknesses—expressions of our sin nature—that we rarely see for ourselves, let alone acknowledge and change.

We grow up in homes with other weak and sinful humans, who sometimes leave us with lasting wounds. We carry those wounds into our marriage determined to avoid further hurt— like a burn patient who holds his burned hand out in front of his body to avoid unintentional contact. In a marriage that protective instinct can keep us stuck, unwilling to brave vulnerability and mutual submission.

Most importantly, few of us remain detached enough to express our concerns to our spouse in a way that they can hear. Instead, our emotions, word choice, tone of voice, and body position transmit a message that our spouses hear as judgmental or superior. Our loved one feels backed into a corner. Instead of hearing and responding, our spouse may hear blame and move into a defensive or counter-accusatory position. Thus begins a cycle that almost never progresses to resolution.

When one spouse consistently deflects blame, the other partner feels more than unheard; they can begin to feel "crazy." It seems as if their version of reality is inaccurate. Though deflection effectively stalls the conflict, it only succeeds until the next crisis begins. In fact deflection can actually entrench the wounded partner's perspective, making forgiveness nearly impossible.

Sometimes, one spouse completely disengages. The problem, they believe, belongs to the unhappy spouse. "I can't help it if you're so unhappy. It's not my problem."

That's a little like ignoring a house fire because the flames began in your husband's workshop. The disengaged spouse doesn't realize that **when one spouse is in crisis, the marriage is in crisis. A marriage always belongs to both partners.** In that way, his problem is your problem. The fire will spread. It's your house; fight the fire.

Few of us are taught effective conflict resolution skills, including anger management, active listening, and clarification—vital skills that help us solve problems that would otherwise destroy our relationships. Very few of us saw these skills successfully modeled in our childhood homes. When addressing any of these issues—

blind spots, woundedness, communication issues—training is the fastest and most direct way to healing. Effective learning takes place most successfully in the safe protection of a professional therapist's office.

In chapter three, I emphasized the benefits of therapy in healing from a traumatic past. At the risk of repeating myself, let me discuss therapy in the context of a difficult marriage.

Getting Professional Help
Going to marriage counseling doesn't appeal to many men. After all, getting help involves a great deal of vulnerability and exposure. It involves admitting your failure, and asking for help. Who wants to go into some stranger's office and admit that your marriage is in difficulty? How do you know whom to trust? What will the therapist do for us anyway? For men especially, preconceived notions based on media parodies can make them very reluctant to engage in the process. Don't let his reluctance stall your efforts to bring healing to your relationship.

At the risk of offending some, I advise those with serious and long-standing marital difficulty to seek the help of a Christian professional rather than the counsel of their pastor. Very few pastors are trained to recognize the complicating physical issues which may add strain to a marriage. Hormone imbalances, addictions, depression, even genuine mental illness—all can play a part in marriage difficulty.

Few pastors can be objective enough to deal with people they know and love. Objectivity is critical to success; without it the offended partner feels isolated in their difficulty, which may cause them to disengage from the process. While isolation may happen in the professional counselor's office, it is far less likely.

Remember that longstanding issues take time to fix. **Rarely does a marriage suffer from a lack of spiritual discipline. Instead,** childhood wounds, repetitive behavior patterns, insecurities, fears and unmet expectations all play a part. Sorting through this kind of pain, teaching and practicing new skills, gradually releasing the couple to grow further on their own—all of these can take enormous amounts of time. Rarely do ordinary pastors have the skills or the time to do this thoroughly.

A professional may be able to recognize areas where physical or psychological impairments are contributing to the conflict. A professional has vast experience with other couples just like you. A trained therapist can help even reluctant people accept, even embrace change. Most pastors face responsibility enough in teaching, preaching and leading their congregation.

The Role of Christian Counseling

In my experience the professional therapist serves at least three critical roles in the marriage relationship. First, the therapist validates the importance of the conflict itself. Generally when two people experience conflict, each tends to minimize the perspective of the other.

Rarely do two people enter therapy willingly. Usually, one partner is the instigator, and the other comes dragging both feet. A good therapist helps the reluctant partner feel as if his perspective is valid. In the process, the therapist also validates the need to address the problem, assuring both partners that it can be solved in a way that leaves them with a better, more mutually satisfying relationship.

During these early hours, a good therapist helps the couple remember why solving the problem is so important. Usually, the couple is encouraged to remember the reasons they chose one another, and to recall the things they value about their partner. This sets the tone for the problem solving and skill training that follows.

In the process of problem solving, a good therapist does not take sides. Instead, he or she guarantees that both spouses feel genuinely listened to, and completely heard by their partner. The therapist guides the husband and wife toward a mutually satisfying resolution. In the end, the therapist works to teach the couple the skills they need to navigate future conflict successfully.

Usually, the therapist is teaching and encouraging good relationship building behaviors while at the same time resolving conflict. Assignments might include hand-holding, daily hugs, daily conversation times—anything that might restore the behaviors that were lost to the conflict. These assignments progress gently, as tolerated, until the silent tension between the two is replaced by loving interaction.

The High Cost of Healing
Whenever I suggest therapy, I am most often met with objections regarding the cost. "We can't afford that. It's too expensive." I understand the objection. Professional counseling is a significant expense. However, the benefit of professional help is worth every penny. **At any cost, a healed marriage is less costly than a divorce leaving wounded partners and devastated children.**

If you cannot afford weekly therapy arrange to go twice monthly. If finances are limited, consider a loan from a family member, getting a second job, or bartering for professional services (even therapists need their oil changed!). Consider sacrificing piano lessons, ballet lessons or music lessons for the kids. Children will likely object at first, but in the end, having a happy family will be worth so much more than a few swimming lessons.

Use your creativity to save money. Perhaps a no-meat meal, babysitting for a friend, or swapping your latte habit for a counseling-savings jar? Your marriage is your most valuable relationship. No second marriage will ever come close. It's worth all your concentration, sacrifice and effort to save it.

In this chapter, we've discussed the importance of a healthy sexual relationship in a healthy marriage. And, we've begun to deal with the issue of longstanding conflict in the difficult marriage. In our next chapter, we'll focus on the ways you can polish up your own conflict resolution skills. In the meantime, think about these questions.

Time for Reflection

> He is the one who gave these gifts to the church. . . that we will be mature and full grown in the Lord. . . Then we will no longer be immature like children. We won't be tossed and blown about by every wind of new teaching. We will not be influenced when people try to trick us with lies so clever they sound like the truth. Instead, we will speak the truth in love, growing in every way more and more like Christ, who is the head of his body, the church.
>
> EPHESIANS 4:11–15

How might this Ephesians passage relate to counseling? Have you ever considered the role of counselor as being a gift to the church?

Is it possible that the counseling profession might be an outgrowth of a combination of spiritual gifts? Which ones might fit? What is the primary goal of the spiritual gifts?

When those gifts help us to become more like Christ, how might that influence:

Our marriage relationship?

Our communication style? (how is Christ's communication different than yours?)

Our interaction with one another? (How is His interaction different than yours?)

Our compassion for one another? (How is His compassion different than yours?)

How might the following scriptures apply to marriage counseling?

> Plans go wrong for lack of advice; many advisers bring success.
> PROVERBS 15:22

> Pride leads to conflict; those who take advice are wise.
> PROVERBS 13:10

> People who despise advice are asking for trouble; those who respect a command will succeed.
> PROVERBS 13:12-14

CHAPTER 6

Minimizing Discord, Maximizing Sex

In our last chapter we talked in detail about why chronic discord is so destructive to the sexual relationship you and your spouse share. We emphasized how important frequent sexual contact is to most husbands. And we discussed how difficult it can be for women to participate in sex when they feel ignored or isolated.

If you and your husband never experience conflict, or if, when you solve problems, you act more like one person than two, this chapter is not for you. You have my permission to move directly to chapter seven.

If, however, your marriage style is more like what the rest of us experience this chapter will give you hope. Whether your conflict style resembles World War I or the Cold War, you can change.

The old adage, "it takes two to tango," is more correct in conflict than in any other human experience. While it takes two to disagree and two to fight, one can change the tone and course of conflict resolution. If you desire, you can be that one.

He Won't Consider Therapy
I've known several women whose husbands refuse therapy. While this may feel like a dead end, it is not. When conflict escalates until it threatens a marriage, the wife can (and should) go to counseling alone. In the safe confines of a neutral party, your

Christian counselor will help you develop skills to cope with the difficulty you face. She can help you grow your communication skills. She can help you develop compassion and understanding for your spouse. Most importantly, she can help you change the dance that you share with your spouse.

Who Me, Dance?

You may not have thought of it this way, but most husbands and wives interact in surprisingly predictable patterns. When he speaks with a particular tone of voice, she reacts in the same way, over and over again. Your decision-making patterns, your schedule planning, even your arguments begin to look very similar to one another.

Whether your relationship is very healthy or in need of a major tune-up, you can be sure that you've developed a pattern of give and take that repeats itself over and over in all the interactions of marital life. That pattern becomes your own relationship "dance."

Anyone who follows contemporary television has noticed today's popular dance competition shows. Watching these, even a non-dancer observes the vast difference between the various steps and rhythms in ballroom dance. The three-beat Waltz can hardly be confused with the latin rhythms of the Tango or Cha-Cha.

As you think about those rhythms and steps, imagine this: Suppose that a costumed couple steps onto the stage as the orchestra begins a beautiful Viennese Waltz. Both partners begin the rise and fall of the three-beat pattern. They circle and turn, when suddenly, without warning, the woman begins to Cha-Cha.

Picture the ensuing chaos as I ask. Can the man continue the Viennese Waltz without interruption? Absolutely not. Without arguing, without contention, simply by changing her steps, the woman has interrupted the dance.

He cannot continue to rise and fall, to turn and bob because she no longer participates in his pattern. Though his steps may not actually become the Cha-Cha, at the very least, he cannot continue as before. At best, he just might begin to follow her steps. Somewhere in the middle, he must opt for change, or someone is going to experience bruised toes.

Meanwhile, the cycle is broken.

In the same way, when a couple is entrenched in patterns of behavior that keep them stuck, patterns that prevent resolution and reconciliation, sometimes a woman's determination to change herself may set the stage for needed breakthrough.

Even when a transformation does not occur, when a husband does not change his own pattern, she is no longer confined to her own destructive thought and behavior patterns. She has, at long last, chosen her own course of action. By doing so, she sets herself free from his destructive or irresponsible behavior.

What Is a "Love Bank?"
In the context of this book, solving conflict is important to protect your sex life. In the context of marriage, solving conflict is important to save your relationship.

When a couple struggles with endless conflict, their behaviors become more and more unhealthy. They begin to experience fewer and fewer positive interactions. According to Dr. Willard Harley, author of *His Needs, Her Needs*, each of us carries an emotional "bank" inside our soul. Whether we are aware of it or not, we keep track of the deposits our spouse makes into our bank. Deposits include all the positive exchanges we have during the day—a kind word, a hug, an encouragment, a helping hand, even an understanding facial expression.

We also keep track of emotional withdrawls. Those withdrawls occur with every negative interaction like harsh words, slights, misunderstandings, and unkept promises.

When withdrawls outnumber deposits, as happens during unresolved or recurring conflict, the status of the relationship deteriorates. The cycle becomes more and more entrenched. Eventually, unless the pattern is broken, some couples even declare that they have stopped loving one another.

Don't let that happen. Work on your conflict resolution skills. Stop the emotional withdrawls that happen when couples fight.

When Porcupines Make Love
Unresolved conflict never stays contained. It bleeds into the rest of a couple's life. During conflict couples begin to assume the worst of one another—even when they are not fighting. They are more easily offended. They are prone to withdraw from one another. They are more likely to blame. What may begin as a tiny frustration grows into full blown discord. For that reason, solving issues as they come up may make the difference between surviving and thriving in your relationship.

When my husband and I experienced the worst of our difficulties, our counselor often repeated this question. "How do porcupines make love?" He always answered his own query, nodding, "Very carefully."

What he meant was that Kim and I had become entrenched in a completely adversarial relationship. No matter what Kim said, I took offense. No matter how he explained himself, I questioned his motives. Believe me, during those years we did resemble porcupines as we bristled and backed away from one another. It was an awful way to live. Yet we couldn't seem to stop ourselves.

Why Resolve Conflict
So, if you struggle, now is the time to build skills. Most people believe that the goal of conflict resolution is simply to resolve conflict. Seems pretty obvious, doesn't it? Get the job done. Make the decision. Choose the wallpaper. Buy the car.

But what if there was something more? **What if one of the goals of conflict resolution were to use the process to grow closer together as a couple? To understand and know one another more intimately?** To express acceptance and compassion to one another? To protect the harmony in your relationship?

What might happen if instead of seeking to out-argue, out-logic, out-wit in a discussion, the entire goal was to really and truly understand the inner world of the person you have married? What if resolving conflict provided a new way to affirm your husband's unique needs or skills or desires? What if problem solving provided you an opportunity to express gratitude, grow closer as a couple or appreciate the life you share together?

If those were the goals behind conflict resolution, the conversations involved might sound completely different, wouldn't they? Instead of loud rebuttals, frequent interruptions and out-and-out put downs, you might hear phrases like these:

- I'd really like to know why you feel that way, honey.
- I can see that this thing is really important to you. Why do you think this crisis is so critical?
- Something that I said has really wounded you. I don't want to do that again. Can you help me understand how my words were so hurtful?
- I never meant to hurt you. How might I have said that in a more productive way?
- Wow, I never understood why a clean house meant so much to you. I get it now.

- I never knew that about your boss. No wonder you hate it when I . . .
- You know, your dad shouldn't have said those things to you. I think you're beautiful. You don't have to buy expensive clothes to convince me.

Time for Reflection

These ideas are more than psychobabble. You can see many of these principles illustrated in scripture. Thinking about marital discord, what instructions do you see in the following passage that might apply?

> So put to death the sinful, earthly things lurking within you. Have nothing to do with sexual immorality, impurity, lust, and evil desires. Don't be greedy, for a greedy person is an idolater, worshiping the things of this world. Because of these sins, the anger of God is coming. You used to do these things when your life was still part of this world. But now is the time to get rid of anger, rage, malicious behavior, slander, and dirty language. Don't lie to each other, for you have stripped off your old sinful nature and all its wicked deeds. Put on your new nature, and be renewed as you learn to know your Creator and become like him. In this new life, it doesn't matter if you are a Jew or a Gentile, circumcised or uncircumcised, barbaric, uncivilized, slave, or free. Christ is all that matters, and he lives in all of us. Since God chose you to be the holy people he loves, you must clothe yourselves with tenderhearted mercy, kindness, humility, gentleness, and patience. . .
> COLOSSIANS 3:5–12

> Therefore I, a prisoner for serving the Lord, beg you to lead a life worthy of your calling, for you have been called by God. Always be humble and gentle. Be patient with each other, making allowance for each other's faults because of your love. Make every effort to keep yourselves united in the Spirit, binding yourselves together with peace.
>
> EPHESIANS 4:1–3

First, what does our earthly nature contribute to discord?

How might truth play into marital discord?

What "old self" habits invade your conflict?

How do humility and gentleness change conflict resolution?

Read the following passages from Proverbs. Under each one, list one trait that might make for less stressful and more fruitful conflict resolution:

Your own soul is nourished when you are kind, but you destroy yourself when you are cruel.
PROVERBS 11:17

The generous prosper and are satisfied; those who refresh others will themselves be refreshed.
PROVERBS 11:25

Those who control their tongue will have a long life; a quick retort can ruin everything.
PROVERBS 13:3

A fool is quick tempered, but a wise person stays calm when insulted.
PROVERBS 12:16

Some people make cutting remarks, but the words of the wise bring healing.
PROVERBS 12:18

If you ignore criticism, you will end in poverty and disgrace; if you accept criticism, you will be honored.
PROVERBS 13:18

Ask the Lord to show you a mental video of your last disagreement with your spouse. Was there something that you wish you had done differently? (Don't focus on what your husband did.) What was it?

Is this a pattern in your arguments?

Have you tried to stop the pattern?

What happened?

Building a Skill Base
Many conflict resolution skills can be learned from a good class or a well-written book. You can learn to choose your timing carefully, to express your concern without blame, and to give your spouse an opportunity to solve your problem with you (rather than blindly accepting your solution). If, in your childhood home, these skills were never modeled for you, learning new skills will take both time and practice. It will feel as foreign as learning to fly. Don't give up too soon. New skills are possible. Lets review some of the most basic rules of conflict resolution:

Fair Fight Rules
- No elevated voices (no yelling).
- No ugly, or inappropriate words.
- No name calling.
- No accusations, such as "you always," or "you never"
- Be cautious in front of children; some disagreements should be private.
- Stay focused on only one issue at a time.
- No withdrawal. No subtle or obvious punishments.
- No physical aggression of any kind. (Watch posture, personal space, gestures, etc.)

Fair Fight Tools
- Ask permission to discuss anything.
- Respect your spouse's timing needs (hungry, tired, etc).

- Ask clarifying questions:
  ("When you say 'redecorate,' what do you mean?")
- Restate your spouse's position.
  (Am I hearing you say . . . ?)
- Listen fully. Make sure you understand your spouse's point of view before stating your own.
- Take a "time out" before things get heated. ("I'm feeling too upset to continue right now. I need a break.")
- Reschedule the discussion when you take a break. ("Can we take this up again after dinner?")
- Brain storm solutions; both spouses needs to participate. (No ideas are off limits. Create a big list first. Then narrow it down to the best ideas before you choose your solution)
- Choose the final solution together.
- Don't be afraid to take as much time as you need to come to a solution you both agree is best.

The Opening Salvo
Imagine two opposing armies lined up for battle. As they face one another across an open field, the tension mounts. Then suddenly the battle begins. How? Someone has shot the opening salvo.

An opening salvo is the first shot from the opposing army. It might come from a shot gun. It might come from a cannon. No matter the weapon, it is the signal for battle to begin. Not surprisingly couples often let verbal opening salvos lead to battles as well. One of the ways that a wise woman can change the dance in marriage conflict is to change the way she responds to an opening salvo. Rather than immediately firing back, a wise woman looks for the meaning behind the salvo.

Practice Makes Perfect
This exercise would be great for a small group: The following quotes might be the "opening salvo" for a enormous fight between husband and wife. Under each quote, write down your answers to the following questions:

- What might be the **real (underlying) problem** or issue?
- What might this spouse **really** want?
- What **question** could the receiving partner ask to clarify the real problem?
- What **solutions** might the couple offer to the problem?

Example 1:
Husband to wife: "I can't stand to spend one more Thanksgiving with your mother!"

Example 2:
Husband to wife: "What is it with all this junk on the floor? All you ever do is spend money!"

Example 3:
Husband to wife: "You're always too tired for sex."

Example 4:
Wife to husband: "You never put your laundry in the hamper."

Understanding Opening Words:
I hope you realize that an opening salvo can be an opportunity for growing closer, or it can lead you into a full-blown fight. How is that possible? In my experience, that first response determines the course of the converstaion. If a partner responds defensively before knowing what is behind that opening salvo, the opportunity for loving communication is all but lost.

For instance, when the husband complains about "all this stuff," most wives would respond with hurt. They interpret his words as a complaint about their housekeeping skills. Hurt, they answer defensively. If she responds to what she **believes** he is complaining about, (without really knowing) she might miss the opportunity to reassure his deepest fears. What else might be going on?

He might be worried about finances. He sees the stuff (toys lying all over the floor) and worries about the credit card bills. In this case, her asking for clarification might lead to a profitable discussion about budgeting or saving.

Or, he might be worried. What if this very afternoon, five of his co-workers were laid off? He sees the toys on the floor and wonders if he'll have a job next week. **If she can ask the right question in spite of such a provocative opening line, she can begin to reassure him about the future instead of fighting about something that isn't really the problem.** With these ideas in mind, perhaps you and your study partners can discuss what responsive questions might have led to greater understanding.

This week, pay attention to the salvos which occur between you and your husband. Think before you respond. Begin with a question (or many questions). Once you have clarification you can begin to work out a solution together.

Time for Reflection

When you argue, do you make it your biggest goal to first fully understand your spouse's point of view—even before you try to solve the problem? What keeps you from doing this?

Do you restate his concerns, so that he knows you have fully listened and understood his point of view before you speak?

What is your typical reaction when an opening salvo makes you feel misunderstood, blamed or accused? What might you do to short circuit that reaction?

Contentedness and Conflict
One of my frustrations with contemporary Christian publishing is the message implied on the back of most self-help books: If you follow these steps, these covers declare, you will experience exactly the results you desire. Those of us who have lived a long life in Christ know better. We cannot control others. We cannot change our children, our church, our husband, our friendships. In truth, we have enough difficulty controling ourselves.

I know. As a child, I lived in a home riddled with conflict. Fights happened regularly. My father relied on his booming voice and cruel words to win discussions. My mother resorted to sarcasm and self depreciation to get her point across. Even today, so many years later, determining to change my conflict resolution behavior feels like pushing a school bus up Mt. Everest. On my own, it's nearly impossible.

Don't forget. Scripture promises that through Jesus we are set free from the power of sin and death. In Jesus, we can experience real change. We can put off the old man, with all of his sinful behaviors and motivations. Through Christ we can put on the new man. We can choose to live holy, contented, spirit-led lives regardless of our current marital situation. Regardless of the choices our husbands make.

When we let discontent take hold in our hearts, we are more likely to fight for what we believe will ease our misery. I ask you, will having more stuff, better stuff, bigger houses, nicer furniture really change anything? Or will it leave you longing for the next "fix?" Could discontent actually fuel the conflict you experience in your marriage?

Contentment is not dependent on our marital status. It does not depend on the happiness of our relationship with our spouse. We can live this life in the heart of the United States or in the poorest neighborhood in Calcutta, India.

Living the victorious life is not dependent on our environment, not contingent on our successful marriage, not related to our bank balance. It depends only on our relationship with Christ and our utter reliance on Him.

Time for Reflection

> How I praise the Lord that you are concerned about me again. I know you have always been concerned for me, but you didn't have the chance to help me. Not that I was ever in need, for I have learned how to be content with whatever I have. I know how to live on almost nothing or with everything. I have learned the secret of living in every situation, whether it is with a full stomach or empty, with plenty or little.
> PHILIPPIANS 4:10–12

Using a score of 1–10, how content are you today?

How do you think contentment and thankfulness might be related?

How often do you find yourself wishing, longing, or thinking about something else—something to have, to buy, to acquire, to accomplish? How often do you wish your husband spoke or acted or thought differently? Does that feed dissatisfaction? What one thing might you change to grow contentment in your life?

If dissatisfaction were a parasite, feeding on your soul, what do you do, or think, or dream about that feeds the parasite? Can you list some of those things here?

At one point in our married life, I chose to throw away (without reading) the many clothing catalogues that appeared in my mailbox. They fueled desire for clothing we could not afford. Ask the Holy Spirit to give you *one* idea, one thing that you can do this week to crowd out disastisfaction, replacing it with contentment in the area of marriage. How will you obey the Spirit?

CHAPTER

The Rich Harvest

So far we've considered God's perspective on our sexuality and tried to understand why our purity matters so much to Him. We've thought about what it means to be fully committed to your exclusive relationship with your spouse. We've eliminated weeds that crowd our sexual garden and considered the many lies that confuse our thoughts and emotions. Most importantly, we've compared those lies to God's Word. Believing the truth, lies no longer hold us.

In the last two chapters, we recognized that a struggling sex life can put additional pressure on our marriage relationship. And, conversely, we discussed the ways that a tough marriage can create a non-existent sex life. In light of a foundering relationship, we considered getting professional help.

At last we've arrived at the point where most sex-education in our culture begins. Now it's time to work on enjoying and growing your sexual relationship. But first, let me tell you a story:

Almost ten years ago my 88-year-old mother went out for her weekly hair appointment, expecting to make a trip to the bank and be home by lunchtime. Newly washed and styled, she stepped off the sidewalk in front of the salon and felt her ankle collapse. With surgery her fractured tibia eventually healed. However, the wound (where her shin broke through her skin) refused to close. Several times during the course of her six month recovery the wound became infected.

During one of these episodes, she came to my house. I cooked for her, took her for walks, and arranged for a home health nurse to change her dressings. Every other day, with my help, Mom took a shower. One day, as she sat on a shower stool, I asked, "Would you like me to wash your back?"

"Ah, that would be heavenly," she said.

I soaped up a bath sponge and began to scrub her back. As I did, I remembered that for almost ten years Mom had lived alone. How long had it been since someone had scrubbed her back? As I washed, I became aware—in an almost otherworldly way— that I was, at that very moment, washing Jesus' back. It was such a holy moment that tears filled my eyes. Silently, I began to worship. I don't think Mom had any idea what was going on behind her.

In that moment, I realized that as I did this kindness for Mom, I had done it for Jesus—exactly as Jesus taught in the book of Matthew.

> "And the King will say, 'I tell you the truth, when you did it to one of the least of these my brothers and sisters, you were doing it to me!'"
> MATTHEW 25:40

It was a truth I'll never forget.

As I've worked through this project, I confess that I've had a similar revelation about my own sexuality. **In the same way that washing my mother's back was an act of service for Jesus, so too is serving my husband sexually. In loving Kim, I love Jesus.**

The Rich Harvest

Like most wives, I have found myself thinking things like, *Now? You want to do that now?* Or worse, *Are you kidding me? You treat me like that all day and you want me to do sex as if nothing has ever happened?* I've been bound up by things like convenience, or fairness, or justification. The idea of serving my husband as an act of worship is new to me. At my age, you'd think I'd know better.

All through scripture we are encouraged to think of others' needs as more important than our own. These passages reflect that truth:

> Don't be selfish; don't try to impress others. Be humble, thinking of others as better than yourselves. Don't look out only for your own interests, but take an interest in others, too.
>
> You must have the same attitude that Christ Jesus had. Though he was God, he did not think of equality with God as something to cling to. Instead, he gave up his divine privileges; he took the humble position of a slave and was born as a human being.
>
> PHILLIPPIANS 2:3–7

I'm not speaking about grumbling sex, resentful sex, or even obedient sex. Truthfully, I don't have it all figured out. When our marriage feels rocky, so does our sex-life. Still, I've finally discovered that there can be something worshipful about sex, about meeting my husband's need with humble generosity. Imagine that! Of course as I please my husband, I enjoy great satisfaction. It's a mystery; I grant you.

Most newlywed couples quickly understand how to create a mutually satisfying sex life. In the early days, they may stumble through the details. However with time most couples iron out their issues. But how do you create a sex life that goes the distance? How can your relationship sustain the energy, interest and vitality to last a lifetime? Can it be done? Absolutely.

The First Enemy: Exhaustion
Just as their sexual expression hits its stride, many young marrieds encounter their first big obstacle. Pregnancy. Even when a new baby is happily anticipated, pregnancy can mark the beginning of sexual complications (more about these later). Pregnancy, of course, leads to the second obstacle—all night care for a newborn, and the subsequent result: exhaustion. Intense days of childcare compound the exhaustion. And then, just as things seem to find their balance, the whole situation succumbs to a second or third or fourth pregnancy.

No question about it, parenthood can wreak havoc on a healthy sex life.

Whether the disruption comes from the complications of pregnancy, persistent hormonal changes, or the exhaustion of months of sleep deprivation, the interruption of a normal, healthy sex life can create sexual stress in most husbands. Not wanting to place additional demands on their exhausted wives, some men back away. His loving consideration of his wife may—even though he tries to avoid it—eventually develop into sexual frustration. On the other hand, a wife's exhaustion can leave her completely uninterested in sex. You can see how an unhealthy cycle might take hold.

Even when couples recover from the interruption of a new baby (and most couples do), the demands of family, school, work, housework, extracurricular activities, and yes, even church responsibilities can crowd out their sexual relationship. As families and children grow, the demands on a parent's time increase as well.

All too often, couples collapse into bed. Exhausted, they turn out the light and are asleep before their hand hits the mattress. It's a common scenario. I've lived it myself.

Exhaustion may be the number one enemy of a healthy sex life. Whether it's caused by the birth of children, over commitment outside the home, busyness, workaholism, too much late night television, hours of Facebook, or intense financial pressure, the result is the same. The sexual relationship ends up crowded into the corner, forgotten for a time.

Why does it happen? Because it can.

A couple can't forget to feed their children, or ignore the bills, or put off going to work. The consequences are too great. But their sexual relationship will live (they believe) for a long time on the back burner. Like so many obligations, couples promise themselves, "We'll get to it eventually." But eventually never comes. Schedules get busier. Obligations grow. Kids face new opportunities. Parents get promotions, deadlines, and new jobs. Don't let exhaustion strip you of the intimacy you and your husband share.

Time for Reflection

What is the longest time you have gone without having sex with your spouse? Why did that happen?

How did that feel to you?

Do you remember how that long abstinence affected your spouse?

Knowing your spouse as you do, what would be his ideal frequency for sex? For you?

Are you open to his preferences? Why or why not? Would meeting his desire change your relationship? How?

Making Sex a Priority
Some couples solve the issue of exhaustion by scheduling sex. These men and women block out their calendars exactly as they would a business meeting. But for others that seems unappealing. Some worry that scheduling sex might feel forced, or won't allow for emotions or fights, or for emergencies. You may rightfully wonder if scheduled sex means an end to spontaneous expressions of love. We humans don't want to feel confined. We may even worry that scheduled sex will feel rote, robotic, or forced.

Most of us want to enjoy the spontaneity of sex. We hope that somehow sex will just happen in the middle of the chaos. After all, it happened that way when we were newlyweds.

To be honest, I'd never considered scheduling sex until I spent time as a mentor mom for Mothers of Preschoolers. There, on a morning where sex was the discussion focus, I discovered that most of the young moms at my table made a habit of scheduling sex with their husbands. Amazed, I asked lots of questions. (Who was mentoring whom?)

The Rich Harvest

I discovered that for most of these moms, scheduling sex helped them to be mentally ready for their husbands. It built anticipation and enjoyment. They found that they were able to arrange the entire day around their sexual appointment—choosing to get homework out of the way earlier, finish baths quickly, even to the point of cooking a dinner that was easier to prepare and needed little clean up. Thus, when these wives crawled into bed, they were not exhausted. Instead, they were expectant and even eager to enjoy private time with their husbands.

Their experience opened my eyes. These young moms aren't the only couples who had stumbled on this solution. Recently, I heard a guest researcher on Doctor Radio, from NYU Medical Center (Sirius Satelite XM) say that **among healthy couples, 80% schedule regular time for sex.**

Scheduled sex isn't the only solution. But using this idea as a jumping off point, other busy wives can enjoy some of the same results. If you aren't interested in a standing "sex date" with your husband, perhaps you'd be willing to take responsibility for one intimate encounter per week. Though it might involve getting a babysitter, or trading an evening of childcare or an over-night visit with a friend, the idea is worth your effort.

You might write out an invitation to "shower night," planning a long, late-evening shower together. Or you might greet him at the back door wearing a surprisingly revealing dress. Imagine how quickly his work tension will slide away!

Of course, many couples schedule private time away from home, going to a hotel or resort. This is great if you have the resources and ability to do so. However, even those who can get away rarely do it with any real regularity. Don't let lack of finances or childcare deter you from regular opportunities for great sex!

Excursions don't have to be expensive. **Consider hosting your soiree in a backyard tent decorated with battery-powered candles. Perhaps you can make a special nest in the family room or outside under the stars.** Perhaps, if you have a friend with a vacation home, you can swap a fully cooked dinner (or two) for a night away.

A woman who creatively and enthusiastically initiates these encounters will be amply rewarded by a grateful husband.
Most men find nothing more thrilling than an eager wife.

By planning time together you'll likely end your evening earlier, getting the kids to bed, pushing aside the endless list of unfinished chores to turn off the television and the laptop. This in itself is helpful. Rather than giving your sexual relationship last place on your agenda, you've moved it to a higher priority where you are both more rested and eager to enjoy yourselves.

Let the important thing (your sexual relationship) be the important thing! Make it a priority. Don't let your sexual life fall to the bottom of your to-do list with gardening and cleaning the garage.

Time for Reflection

> I am my lover's, and he claims me as his own. Come, my love, let us go out to the fields and spend the night among the wildflowers. Let us get up early and go to the vineyards to see if the grapevines have budded, if the blossoms have opened, and if the pomegranates have bloomed. There I will give you my love.
> SONG OF SOLOMON 7:10–12

The Rich Harvest

The Bride in Song of Solomon planned a sexual encounter for her groom. When was the last time you planned a sexual event for your spouse? How did it turn out?

Would you change anything about the encounter? How might that have changed the results?

If things went badly, would you be willing to try something else, something less risky?

Talk to your husband about scheduling sex. What does he think?

What adjustments might you make to be successful?

What about the kids? How can you adjust your "private time" to the kid's schedule? What about the evening? While they are at youth group? On Scout night? During soccer practice? Or Awana? Think together. Write down several ideas:

How might you arrange a weekend away? Would you be willing to make it a priority? Would your husband? Where might you go? How might you make it financially possible?

If you asked your husband to join you, beginning with the phrase, "I'd love to have a whole weekend away to make love as much as we want," what do you think he might say?

Your Brain: Your Largest Sex Organ
In my conversations with women, I've discovered that many of us struggle with our lack of sexual interest. We want to be there for our husbands, but we don't have his level of eagerness. It's more than fatigue. Because women aren't made like men, we feel unable to fix the problem.

While women will never be as focused as men sexually, women must remember that their biggest sex organ lies in their cranium, right between their ears! Just by thinking about sex, initiating and planning a sex date with our spouses, we effectively build up anticipation that can make us—yes even women—both more enthusiastic about and more fulfilled by our sexual encounter. When we use our brains to build a healthy expectation and eagerness for our husbands it will serve us well.

The Second Enemy: Silence
The first time I taught this material, each student completed a confidential questionnaire. I wanted to know what sexual wounds plagued the individuals in our group. I wanted to know why they took the class, and what they hoped to accomplish. Most of all, I wanted to avoid further hurt.

I asked, "How comfortable are you talking about your sexuality?" Imagine my surprise when nearly every student rated themselves as strongly uncomfortable talking about this subject. As a teacher, I'd looked forward to thought provoking discussions about important issues. I assumed, wrongly it turns out, that anyone who might take this kind of class would want to talk about these ideas.

But that wasn't the only problem. The other, more subtle issue is this: If women have difficulty speaking to one another about sex, (where there is little risk and no marital discord at stake), was there any sexual discussion going on between these women and their husbands? Any feedback? Any appreciation? I wondered.

If women (who are generally more verbal than most men) hesitate to discuss these issues, how much more hesitant are those less verbal men? For many men, this kind of conversation threatens their sexual prowess. Their manhood is at stake when it comes to satisfying their wife. Any suggestions or requests can easily be mistaken for criticism. Criticism can feel like failure, which causes hurt. When wounded, most of us pull back.

In order to cultivate a healthy and satisfying sexual relationship, couples must be able to talk about what they experience together.

And, of course, a woman must be able to express her concerns and desires in ways that don't leave her husband feeling inadequate or discouraged.

Sexuality can be so difficult to talk about that many couples simply won't try. Instead, they try to telegraph their needs to one another. Sometimes, wives resort to sarcasm. Husbands resort to belittling, or name-calling. Women wish he would just "do it this way." Men wish for more sex, and instead of talking openly, they make a few advances, and when rebuffed retreat into themselves or their hobbies.

Why is talking about sex so difficult? Perhaps because doing so requires such intense vulnerability. Asking for what we desire gives our spouse the power to deny our wishes. In some cases, expressing our desires may leave us open to judgement. That can cause intense anxiety. Speaking about sex can be embarrassing.

After all, most of us grew up in a world where the only sex talk we heard was crass or immoral. Because it is such a personal issue, none of us have had this kind of conversation modeled for us. Thus we wade into this subject without a clue as to how to begin. **If conversations about housework or child rearing are already difficult, you can imagine how frightening a conversation about sex might feel.**

Part of the problem is that we don't truly know one another sexually. For instance: Do you know what is most stimulating for your spouse? Is he visual? Or does he love to be touched? Does he love candlelight? Or mirrors? What is his favorite position? What does he love most for you to do to his body?

Have you asked him? Or have you just guessed based on years of experience? Certainly, careful observation can be a wise teacher. However, **why wait years to discover what pleases your husband when a simple question may give you the best and most direct answer?**

The Rich Harvest

Do you see how gentle questions might become the simplest of beginnings? Ask. You needn't ask in the midst of passionate activity. Instead, when you are happy and alone together, begin with something like this:

> "I really want you to enjoy our love-making. So I've been wondering. When you think about having sex with me, what's your favorite way for it to happen?"
>
> Or this: "Where do you love being touched the very most?"
> Or this: "What could I do for you sexually that would really please you?"

If he has trouble answering, try giving him some options.
- "Would you like me to initiate more often?"
- "Would you like to have me wear fancy lingerie to bed?"
- "Which is your very favorite position for sex? Why is that?"
- Try an open-ended question: "Fill in the blank. When it comes to sex, I love it when you _____."

You may be surprised at what you hear. By expressing desire to give him pleasure and providing a safe opening for the conversation, you may find that he responds with similar questions. This might lead to an opportunity to share your dreams and wishes. If not, you might begin by expressing your appreciation for some recent time together. I was able to do that recently.

Not long ago, I invited my husband to share our jetted bathtub by candlelight. Normally, the tub isn't his domain. He's a guy's guy, a shower guy. What surprised me was that we lounged in the tub for a couple of hours and talked. Yes, we ended the evening with our own little fireworks show. But I was most encouraged by that time together in the tub.

When I spoke with him before dinner the next night I told him, "I loved our time together last night. It was so great. You know what I loved best?" He had no idea. "I just felt so listened to. It was so great to have your undivided attention while I shared what was going on in my world."

I wanted him to know how thankful I felt for our time together. And because my hubby is a very bright fella, I expect he's thinking about ways that he can repeat his performance. He's human. We all like a little appreciation!

Almost forty years ago my Psych 101 professor taught, "A behavior that is reinforced will be repeated." When I was raising children, the experts used to say, "Catch the little guy doing something right and make a big deal over it." Husbands aren't so different. They like reinforcement too.

I rediscovered this truth quite by accident. Once, during our intimate time together, I said, "I love it when you are all showered and smell so great." I wasn't trying to manipulate my husband. I was just expressing my pleasure. To my surprise, he remembered that comment. Now in the evening, he sometimes comes to me with a smile and a twinkle in his eyes, saying, "I just had a shower . . ." I know what he has in mind.

Suppose you'd like your husband to spend more time caressing you. Or maybe you'd like to have him get out of the same old "sex-routine." That kind of request could feel like criticism. Or, it could sound like adventure.

In his book *Sheet Music*, Dr. Lemen advises his readers to begin with this little phrase, **"You know what I've always wanted to try?"** Instead of feeling corrected, your spouse will feel inspired. Perhaps you might try these kinds of suggestions:

- "I've always wanted to try a foot massage by candlelight."
- "I've always wondered what it would feel like to focus on kissing for fifteen whole minutes. . ."

- "I've always wanted to see how much time we could spend caressing one another before the main event. What if we put it off until we were both just chomping at the bit?"

Dr. Lemen's suggested phrasing makes it clear that you want to engage, that you are all in, that you are eager to please and be pleased. It may be the magic means to bring your desires to your husband's attention without having him feel like a failure.

Time for Reflection

How does the idea of talking about sex with your spouse feel? Have you tried? What happened?

Which of the questions in this chapter would you feel most comfortable asking? When will you talk about it together?

Is there something "off" about how you connect with your spouse sexually? What is it?

Can you think of a question (or two) that might initiate a discussion without blame or fault-finding? Write them here.

When was the last time you expressed gratitude for an enjoyable sexual experience? Even if speaking about sex is difficult, can you let your husband know that you appreciate his efforts?

Self- Stimulation
I'd like to take a moment here to talk a bit about something rarely discussed in Christian circles. The world calls it masturbation. A better term might be self-stimulation. It fits into this discussion of learning to grow your sexual life because self-stimulation has the power to both enhance and destroy a couple's sexual intimacy.

When I was a young bride, the topic of masturbation was relegated entirely to men and young boys. In general, the admonition was simple. "Don't." Today, though, the concern about masturbation has many facets.

Today masturbation is frequently connected with the use of pornography. In that context, a man's self-stimulation actually replaces interaction with his wife. Masturbation becomes more and more habitual, eventually becoming the preferred method of pleasure. Many women whose husbands are involved in pornography report that their husband's interest in normal sex has diminished or even disappeared, leaving the wife without a healthy means of sexual expression or satisfaction.

In cases where self-stimulation replaces interaction with your spouse, I'd advise both men and women to avoid masturbation. Remember scripture admonishes us to meet one another's sexual needs.

However, for the young, inexperienced bride, the one who has never been touched, who has never experienced sex, this issue may be complicated. How can she teach her husband to please her if she has no idea what feels good or uncomfortable or painful? In this case, it might actually be helpful for a young woman to explore her own body, to discover where tender touches are pleasing and how her body reacts to different kinds of touch. This can be done in a variety of settings—in a relaxing warm bath, or alone with music and privacy. If done with the intent of helping her husband to grow their sexual bond rather than substituting for his interaction, self-stimulation may actually help to accomplish these godly goals.

There are other ways to grow your sex life. Some are common sense; others will surprise you.

The Third Enemy: A Critical Heart
Earlier, we looked at this scripture. This time, we will see it from a different point of view.

> My lover is dark and dazzling,
>   better than ten thousand others!
> His head is finest gold, his wavy hair is black as a raven.
> His eyes sparkle like doves
>   beside springs of water;
> they are set like jewels
>   washed in milk.
> His cheeks are like gardens of spices giving off fragrance.
> His lips are like lilies,
>   perfumed with myrrh.
> His arms are like rounded bars of gold, set with beryl.
> His body is like bright ivory,
>   glowing with lapis lazuli.
> His legs are like marble pillars
>   set in sockets of finest gold.
> His posture is stately, like
> the noble cedars of Lebanon.
> His mouth is sweetness itself;
>   he is desirable in every way.
> Such, O women of Jerusalem,
>   is my lover, my friend.
>   SONG OF SOLOMON 5:10–16

The woman in Song of Soloman demonstrates an important aspect of an exciting sex life. She appreciates her spouse, rehearsing his positive, attractive qualities even when he is not present. She allows her thought life to "rev-up" her sexuality. By focusing her thoughts on her husband, and yes, on his beautiful body, she prepares herself to respond sexually when he is present.

You may argue that your husband is no beauty—at least not Soloman's kind of beauty. That may be true. Remember in Soloman's day, men didn't use deodorant. They didn't shower daily. Their hair was not styled. Their beards were not short. This bride could have complained about her smelly, hairy husband. But she chose instead to focus on his positive qualities, rehearsing them in her mind. Doing so, she builds appreciation and loyalty to her man. She is wisely growing her sexual bond with him.

You may not have thought about the power of appreciation. By considering your husband's strengths, being aware of his gifts, by practicing gratitude, you too might grow your sex life.

The Fourth Enemy: An Unhealthy Lifestyle
In our next lesson we'll discuss the ways that our aging bodies may betray our sexuality. Of course, aging can't be avoided. But did you know that by keeping your body healthy, you can make a huge difference in your sex life? Of course this is true for both men and women. Let's talk about some of the important points.

Exercise
Authorities agree that women who exercise experience greater satisfaction during sexual intercourse than non-exercisers (though the source of this effect has been difficult to identify). In one study, (published in *Eur J Appl Physiol.* 2003 Sep;90(1-2):199-209. Epub 2003 Jul 9), researchers discovered that bloodstream testosterone levels rise after exercise. Though levels did not remain elevated for a more than 24 hours, the increase was sig-

nificant (20% at two hours). Since testosterone plays a vital part in a woman's sexual desire and response, this may be part of the explanation for increased satisfaction among exercisers.

However, a more subtle connection between exercise and great sex may be found in the general effects of regular exercise. According to the American Heart Association, regular exercise helps reduce stress. Because exercise helps your brain produce endorphins, it may also result in better moods and a general sense of well being.

Exercise gives us time to reflect, time to reenergize. It can increase strength, flexibility and endurance. Exercise gives us a healthy heart, lungs and circulatory system—all of which enhance our ability to enjoy vigorous sex. Any of these exercise benefits can produce a positive effect on our love life.

I know that I feel better when I exercise; working out lifts my mood, helps me to sleep better and to maintain an ideal weight. When my youngest was three, I committed to walk together with a small group of friends. We crept out of bed before our husbands left for work, walking five days a week. We've done it now for almost twenty-five years. Though I do additional exercise, this is my base routine. It has made a huge difference in my life. I began it for my body. I continue for my soul. These women have become my soul sisters.

While exercise may boost our sexual self confidence, in men, it actually enhances the process that enables the penis to respond to stimulation. Overweight men are more likely to experience difficulty obtaining and maintaining an erection (for a wide variety of reasons). If you can find a way to exercise with your husband (or to encourage him to exercise), you may create the kind of vascular changes that enable you both to enjoy a long and healthy sex life!

A Healthy Diet
While our culture equates diet issues only with weight control and sex appeal, there may be a far more important issue at stake. A healthy diet may actually influence a woman's ability to enjoy her sexuality for a lifetime.

According to the Mayo Clinic (http://www.mayoclinic.com/health/belly-fat/WO00128) all body fat produces estrogen. A menstruating female produces most of her estrogen in her ovaries. While estrogen itself is good, **excess levels of estrogen produced by excess body fat may throw off the female hormone balance** (just as fat-produced estrogen throws off the hormone balance in men).

For instance, in a woman who still menstruates, the additional estrogen produced by excess body fat may diminish (by proportion) her available levels of testosterone. Without testosterone, she may actually experience diminished libido, decreasing her interest in sex and her ability to respond sexually.

Diabetes and Great Sex
Diet, weight and sexual satisfaction are all critically interrelated when it comes to the development of Type II Diabetes. Diabetes is the name given to the condition where a person's blood carries too much sugar (and sugar is unable to enter into the body's cells). Over time, when the condition continues without treatment, high blood pressure, heart disease, vascular compromise and even blindness can result. Eventually vascular disease can result in neuropathy, ulcers, infections and even amputation of the feet and legs.

Diabetes influences your sexuality as well. **Women with Type II Diabetes experience less interest in sex and less ability to achieve orgasm.** This is complicated by the fact that many medications used to treat these patients (and its accompanying complications, such as heart disease, high blood pressure, high lipid levels, etc.), may actually work to decrease sexual desire.

By eating a healthy diet, you provide your body with the nutrition to be active both physically and sexually. At the same time a diet rich in complex carbohydrates, balanced by good sources of protein, vegetables, and high quality fats will prevent the kinds of chronic illnesses that rob you of a satisfying sexual relationship. Eat well. Your body and your spouse will thank you!

In general, experts agree that **maintaining an ideal body weight is critical to preventing the development of diabetes.** Diabetes occurs when the body's need for insulin outstrips the pancreas' ability to produce it. This can happen in two important ways.

For every pound of body weight you carry, your body requires a corresponding volume of insulin. By decreasing your weight you decrease the amount of insulin your body needs. This is the reason that **Type II Diabetics who lose weight often return blood sugar levels to normal**. By maintaining an ideal weight, they put their diabetes into remission and are able (under a doctor's supervision) to go off their diabetes medication.

The reverse is also true. When a person gains excess weight, he increases his need for insulin. When the body can no longer produce enough, diabetes (or high blood sugar levels) results. (To be fair, it is also possible for some patients to develop Type II Diabetes for no discernable reason. In fact, 1 out of 5 Type II diabetics are of normal weight.)

The second way that people may develop diabetes is by eating foods that demand large amounts of insulin to process. These foods (high in immediately available sugars, like white potatoes, white bread, cakes, soda and candy) cause a rapid rise in blood sugar, and the body, in a desperate effort to control sugar levels, dumps high volumes of insulin into the blood.

Eventually, this diet pattern can cause the pancreas (which produces insulin) to fatigue, and the amount of available insulin decreases or even disappears altogether. Eventually sky rocketing blood sugar levels result in a diagnosis of diabetes.

Diabetes presents a critical sexual complication for men as well. According to British research, 35 to 75% of men with diabetes also suffer from erectile dysfunction. If your husband is newly diagnosed with diabetes, making lifestyle changes will be difficult for him. You can encourage his commitment to healthy living by gently reminding him of the risk of diabetic impotence. For most men few issues carry more weight.

For the sake of your sex-life, eating well and avoiding diabetes is an investment in your life-long pleasure.

A Fifth Enemy: Distraction
Often women feel an intense need for secure privacy during sex. For these women, the very possibility of being discovered by wandering children or interrupted by the hotel housekeeping staff can completely disrupt her ability to enjoy time with her husband. If this is your concern, ask your husband to help you secure your bedroom door. A simple lock, (for instance a hook and eye) placed high on the bedroom door, can provide all the security you need.

For other women, and I list myself among these, focus plays a key role in their ability to enjoy sex. For these, a television set, a ringing telephone or even music can prevent the concentration needed to achieve orgasm. If you are among these women, ask your husband if you can disconnect the phone, turn off the television and the music. If, by concentrating, you can more fully enjoy your time together, your husband will be more than happy to cooperate.

A Sixth Enemy: Boredom
If you believe today's movies and television, the only way to add

spice or new interest to a life-long relationship is to add darker, dirtier sexual behaviors. Some even advise adding pornography or additional sexual partners. Don't fall for this foolishness. **You don't have to wind yourself into unnatural shapes, engage in bizarre or hurtful role play, or wear silly costumes to enliven your sexual relationship. Instead, just by committing to please your spouse, you will discover new and fresh ways to enjoy your time together.**

A fresh approach: Creativity
One way that you can add enjoyment to your time together is to play games while giving them a sexual overtone. You don't have to play strip poker, but you could play Strip Name That Tune. You can enjoy board games in playful ways. Or you can be open to new locations. Enjoy one another on a boat. On a private beach. In your back yard. You can add sensual touches to your play. Try silk sheets, or silk boxers for your husband. Try botanical massage oils with enticing fragrances. Use frosting or whipped cream to paint pictures on one another.

Women have a unique advantage when it comes to adding pleasure to their sex life. Most men are visually stimulated. I encourage you to consider adding small bits of enticing lingerie to your collection. These need not be expensive. Check the sale racks. Buy off season. Frequent the discount stores. I once wrapped a very tiny piece of lingerie in a ring box and slipped it under my husband's pillow. He was thrilled! It made for a fun evening together.

If you are willing to consider any idea *and* you give one another permission to discard activities that aren't gratifying or mutually comfortable, you will discover all kinds of new ways to enjoy your sexuality together.

Time for Reflection:

Have you ever considered exercise and diet a means to a better sex life? Does this make exercise more attractive to you?
Do you get regular exercise? What do you do? For how long? How often?

If you haven't yet given yourself this exercise gift, how might you begin? Could you ask your husband to help you accomplish this goal?

Be honest: How healthy is your diet? What **one** thing might you improve? (Don't get sucked into a long list of changes. Focus on adding one behavior at a time).

Experts agree that it is difficult to find healthy meals away from home. How many fast food meals do you eat every week? Could you change this by preparation? Planning?

The Rich Harvest

Have you calculated your body mass index (BMI)? You can easily do so by looking up BMI on the web. There are hundreds of sites which will calculate your numbers for you. All you need are your current height and weight. Are you within the ideal weight range for your height?

On a scale of one to ten, rate your need for privacy before and during sex. Does this make frequent sex difficult for you to enjoy together? What could you do to feel more secure?

Have you ever considered that sexual time together could be playful? How playful have you been in the past?

List four playful ideas that you might try with your husband this coming month:

Good Sex Makes a Good Marriage Better
Certainly no one believes that great sex will solve every marital problem. However, great sex goes a long way toward making a good marriage better. In this chapter we've talked about the important ways a woman can enhance her sexual relationship with her husband. Perhaps for the next thirty days, you can make one of these ideas your goal:

- Find new ways to make sex a priority.
- Talk openly about your mutual sexual needs and desires.
- View diet and exercise as an investment in your sex life.
- Create a safe, private environment to express your sexuality.
- Think creatively about new ways to enjoy sexual time together.

In the next chapter, you'll begin to think about the things that may keep you from enjoying your best sex ever.

CHAPTER 8

Considering Inhibitions

Any discussion about amping up sexual pleasure would be incomplete without some discussion of personal hangups, or inhibitions. Whether you feel uncomfortable dressing in front of your husband, or awkward having sex with the lights on, these inhibitions can keep you from reaching your full sexual potential as a couple.

Inhibitions—those inner restrictions that keep you from enjoying a specific sexual activity—can come from anywhere. They don't limit themselves to dirty or questionable behaviors. Sometimes, they defy logic. Often they arrive with intense emotions.

One of mine came from a childhood admonition. My mother said, "Good girls don't chase boys." She believed that men despise women who pursue them. She thought that my interest in any particular man was best expressed more subtly than by calling them on the telephone or asking them out on dates. I think there was some wisdom in her philosophy.

But my mother's guidance stuck long after I married. Because of her advice I have felt awkward initiating sex with my own husband. In my mind, I still struggle with being a "good girl."

After so many years together, I've finally learned that my husband loves it when I initiate. When I do, he feels wanted, desired, important—all messages I want to convey. Providing him with that kind of pleasure is worth understanding and rejecting the source of my own inhibition.

Your past can affect your inhibitions positively as well. One of my friends grew up in a Christian home with a mother who taught sex education. As a child in her home, talking about sexuality was normal. I imagine that she has very little inhibition when it comes to pleasing her husband. My friend entered marriage with a freedom few of us enjoy.

Instead, most of us bring distorted inhibitions to our relationships. We've seen inappropriate images. We carry past hurts and abuses into the bedroom. A woman who has experienced molestation, sexual abuse, or even rape may feel very differently about some sexual behaviors than a woman who has not.

Discussing Shame
Do you remember the Genesis description of Adam meeting Eve? In that story scripture tells us they were both naked, yet not ashamed. In that one phase, Moses conveys much about the soul of both Adam and Eve. He is speaking about more than physical self-confidence. Moses tells us that both Adam and Eve were at ease in their inner soul. They were not ashamed to be fully themselves, exposed both physically and emotionally. That passage brings us to the issue of shame.

What is shame? In spite of the old expression "shame on you," shame is not really about behaving badly. It is not about what we have done. **Shame is a deep seated sorrow about who we are—about our inadequacy, our history, our personhood.** Shame is not the same as guilt. Guilt is about what we have done. Guilt is a good thing; guilt drives us to God, knowing that God is the only solution for our sin problem. Guilt can and should lead to repentance and restoration.

Shame drives us to hide. It breaks down relationships and puts distance between husbands and wives. It drives us to pretend to be someone we are not. It pushes us to cover up our true selves, our real likes and dislikes, our true emotions. It allows us to present a lie to the world. This is who I am, we declare, when in truth we are something much different, more complex, more genuine.

Time for Reflection

Using this definition of shame, are you ashamed of who you are?

Are you ashamed of your body?

Are you ashamed of your lack of accomplishments? Lack of talent? Lack of giftedness?

Are you ashamed of your past? Of what has happened to you or of what you have done in the past?

Banishing Shame

Let me give you some wise advice: If shame shows up in your bedroom, it will destroy your sexual relationship with your spouse. It will inhibit your joy. It will limit your expression of love. It will steal your confidence. It might even lead you to refuse the love your spouse offers.

Shame is like mold. After hurricane Katrina destroyed parts of New Orleans it was mold, flourishing in the moist post-flood environment, that made homes unrestorable. Sometimes invisible, mold grew behind sheetrock, on wood framing, in spaces that could not be seen. Homes which had survived that brutal storm had to be destroyed because of a toxic fungus. Like mold, shame will creep into your inner spaces. Equally toxic, shame will eat away at your psyche, leaving you hiding in some dark corner.

If shame shows up in your bedroom, it might be time to do something about it. Talk to your pastor. Seek Counseling. Ask an older woman to work with you on this issue. You are never to old to be free!

Other Inhibitions

As you try to grow your sexual relationship with your husband, you may discover inner limits that keep you from moving forward. Now is the time to make a commitment to willingly consider your own inhibitions. Ask yourself where they came from? What do you believe about the issue or behavior? Where do your conclusions come from?

Examine your inhibitions in the light of day. If your husband suggests something that makes you pause, ask yourself why. Before you reject his idea, try to get underneath your resistance. See if you can trace your feelings all the way to the memory or the beliefs behind your response. See if there is something you can do to clear up your resistance.

Some inhibitions, like the one I brought from my childhood, are simple enough to reject. Others caused by trauma or abuse may require more work. Consider what you might do to minimize the embarrassment and resistance you feel.

Perhaps, as you reconsider that vivid memory and tell yourself the truth about what happened, you can experience forgiveness and release from those feelings. If someone wounded you, begin to take steps toward forgiving the offender. If you were involved in inappropriate sexual behavior, ask God for forgiveness. Study passages that remind you of God's great and forgiving heart. Ask Him to help you look at your memories from His point of view. Begin to tell yourself the truth about what happened, even if the sin involved was your own.

Remember all have sinned and fallen short of God's glory (Romans 3:23). You and I are just two among the great mass of human sinners! God has made a way of forgiveness (Romans 3:22), that enables you to face God with a clean conscience (Romans 3:26). As a forgiven daughter of the King, perhaps it is time to forgive yourself and reclaim the loving sexual relationship God had in mind for you when he designed your husband.

Doing this, even at the expense of facing painful memories, would greatly please your husband. Isn't loving him worth stretching yourself? Is it possible that this work might free you from the chains of the past or fears of the present?

All of us want freedom from unhealthy inhibitions. As we work toward freedom, we must remember the purpose behind our sexual relationship. God has given us our sexuality to build the bond between us. Therefore, when inhibitions come between a husband and wife, couples would best reject any activity that—for whatever reason—might disrupt that bond.

When you are both calm and relaxed, consider asking your spouse to set you free from any sexual expectation that you cannot fulfill—at least for now. What is impossible today may not be so difficult tomorrow. We can all grow and change, learning to please our spouses and discovering new freedom as we do.

Time for Reflection

Are there things that your husband has asked of you that make you uncomfortable?

How did you respond? Thinking about that now, would you respond the same way? What might you have said?

Where did your discomfort come from? Can you identify it? Can you commit to pray about it?

Does this chapter remind you of issues or events from your past? Do you need to work through forgiving someone? Do you need to reaffirm your need for God's forgiveness? Will you commit to this process?

Is there a way that you might work toward that sexual behavior or activity in a slower or more comfortable way? List the progression here:

Oral Sex
Advice about inhibitions should probably touch on this sensitive subject, one that so few discuss, even today.

When I was a young bride, I was asked to be an assistant for a woman's Bible study. My only job, I was told, was to take roll. In spite of inexperience and fear, I agreed. **On the first day of class** (I don't remember which book of the Bible we were studying), **the teacher managed to spend the entire class telling those women that oral sex was an abomination and all who practiced it were going straight to hell.**

By the next week, I'd been promoted to Bible study leader (Never did a more unprepared teacher lead a class). At the time, I was shocked that any woman would even speak about such a thing in public. Even as a very young Christian, I realized that the previous teacher had formed an opinion about a subject for which the Bible itself was largely silent. You'll find no clear biblical restriction about oral sex. Those who preach such restrictions do so by creating their own definitions. They lump oral sex into "abominations," which are never specified.

Instead, I have read the work of some Old Testament scholars (those who read and study in the original language) who believe there are references to oral sex in the Song of Solomon. Those passages have been purified, they believe, by translators who chose more acceptable terms for such intimate interaction.

I don't have the skills to judge the validity of these claims. At the very least, one might apply logic to the question. If kissing lips is permissible (though the human mouth is hardly clean), and kissing other parts of the spouse's body is also permissible (the groom is found with his head resting between the bride's breasts in Song of Solomon), does it not also follow that kissing the most sensitive parts of the body (where it might give the most pleasure), might also be permissible? I think so.

"Oral sex" is a contemporary term. Recently it has grown negative, even obscene connotations. It has experienced demonization, from presidential infidelity to current prime time television. It has been objectified and made vile by the most horrific of slang. However, public perception should never determine our values or behavior.

I believe that these kisses and touches—of the most intimate and tender kind—can provide intense pleasure.

In some circumstances, when surgeries and illness rob us of normal sexual expression, these kisses and touches may be the only available means of sexual contact between loving spouses. Such is the case with one couple I know struggling with the effects of a devestating spinal cord injury. At other times, for instance when hormones or aging body parts fail us, the added intensity of oral sex can make the difference between response and passivity.

If your spouse asks you to participate, consider your response carefully. If you hesitate, ask yourself why. Are you held back by your own inhibition? Have you experienced abuse that makes the idea repellant to you? Or have you been taught, as that Bible Study leader taught so many years ago, that this particular sexual expression was inappropriate or even sinful?

There is one caveat when considering oral sex. Current medical research connects oral sex and the transmission of the

human papiloma virus. Variations of this virus are responsible for many diseases, including genital warts and cervical cancers. It may cause some penile and anal cancers as well. Most recently this virus has been linked to oral and pharyngial (throat) cancers, which are believed to be passed on during oral sex. This virus may be behind the dramatic rise in diagnosis of such cancers.

If you or your spouse have been sexually active with other partners, you may now carry the HPV virus. Of the more than thirty kinds of HPV, many will clear the body within two years. Others linger on. You may want to speak to your health care provider about the wisdom of the HPV vaccine, or about appropriate testing for the HPV virus. Whatever your decision regarding oral sex, it should be informed by the possibility of viral transmission. Of course, couples who have never had sex with any other partner are not likely to carry or transmit the virus.

If you wish to move past your inhibitions about oral sex, proceed slowly. Do so as a willing gift to your spouse. You may find that your gift gives one or both of you newfound delight. Don't let your preconceived notions and inhibitions rob you!

Oral Sex and Pregnancy
Though oral sex is not prohibited during pregnancy, medical professionals do give this advice: Do not blow air into the vagina during pregnancy. Doing so might introduce air through the cervix into the uterine area, which eventually enters the bloodstream. These air bubbles, called air emboli, can travel to the lungs, heart and brain, causing immediate death to both mother and child.

Anal Sex
While anal sex has no direct restriction in scripture (for heterosexual couples), I would like to discuss this from the point of view of a health care professional. Here are some considerations that might aid you in making decisions about this sexual activity:

First, the lining of the anus is vastly different from the skin, or lining, of the vagina. Where the vagina has mucosal cells that produce lubrication, the anus has none. Anal dryness, combined with its thinner strucure make the anus more vulnerable to tearing during intercourse.

Healing of anal tears can be problematic because the anus is home to many bacteria whose presence may actually slow the repair process. In addition, tears may allow gastrointestinal bacteria to enter the bloodstream causing septicemia (the presence of pus-forming bacteria in the bloodstream resulting in a full body infection). I know one ICU nurse who believes most of her septicemia cases originate from anal sex. In cases where bacterial or viral organisms causing sexually transmitted disease may be present (Such as the AIDS or hepatitis virus), the risk of transmission in anal sex is very high, much higher than in vaginal sex.

The bacteria of the colon persist in vast quantities in the anus. While those bacteria are healthy and necessary in the colon, they frequently cause disease when introduced to the vagina (where they do not ordinarily reside). The most common cause of bacterial infection in the vagina is colonic bacteria. The easiest route of transmission is anal penetration followed by vaginal penetration. In this way, even in a loving life-long marriage, anal sex can lead to illness.

While anal sex can be very pleasing to men, it is far less so for their wives. Research indicates that about 80% of women need clitoral stimulation to achieve orgasm. Because the anus does not have the same degree of innervation as the vagina and clitoral region, it is rarely as gratifying for women (as men). For all these reasons, I would advise couples to carefully consider the high risks and limited benefits of anal sex. If couples choose to participate, lubricants can reduce the chance of physical damage to the rectum. Condoms may reduce disease transmission, especially if they are removed before vaginal penetration.

Life Together Without Sex?

Some young moms tell me they have no interest in a vibrant sex life. Their children, jobs, housework, and church activities demand all their energy. Some honestly believe that they don't have any real sexual needs of their own. They tell me they can "take it or leave it."

I understand. A drowning woman is not likely to worry about having unfulfilled sexual needs either. Her only concern is to make it to the surface of the water and keep herself afloat for as long as possible—hopefully until someone rescues her.

For many young mothers life feels remarkably like drowning.

As I think about the incredible gift of sexual expression, and the strength of the bond it creates between husband and wife, I believe that it is a vital need for every bride—whether or not she recognizes it. Though she may not feel an obvious, demanding, physical need, even a drowning woman needs to feel profoundly connected with her husband. The intimacy, touch, and emotional high of sexual expression all provide that gift.

When that deep connection created by sexual expression is not present, a woman can grow irritable and progressively distant— even when she is the one who has pulled back from sex. She may become highly critical, even unreasonable in her expectations. And, as we have discussed, her husband's concrete and physiological frustration with a non-existant sex life may drive him toward sinful behavior. Though his choice about how he responds is not her responsibility, she *is* responsible for the Biblical admonition to meet his sexual needs.

It is a wise woman who understands and cultivates her own sexual needs. She thinks about what kinds of sexual expression she finds most pleasurable and pursues those activities with her husband. If hugs and touches and kisses are especially gratifying, she makes sure that these play a major part in her sexuality.

If time away for slow and uninterrupted sexual expression are key, then she takes responsibility to make sure that these activities happen with some frequency. If she has special requests, she makes these known to her husband—whether it be for a quiet location, a freshly showered spouse, or a lengthy after-glow. She recognizes that meeting her own sexual needs with gentle and open requests will, in the end, help her to meet her husband's sexual needs as well.

A wise woman considers satisfying her husband more than just an obligation, but rather a gift she gives herself. A woman who loves the Lord considers her gift to her husband an act of worship. She takes care of her body, seeking help at the first sign of illness or dysfunction. She arranges her life so that the important things take their important place. She chooses not to let life run her, but instead restricts or eliminates the activities that rob her of this vital connection to her husband.

Are you a wise woman?

CHAPTER 9

The Body Betrayed

Most of the time, healthy, loving partners can enjoy a fulfilling sexual relationship for a lifetime. However, in this fallen world, sometimes illness, injury, or cancer may interfere. Even normal and expected life situations can sometimes get in the way of a happy sex life. When pregnancy, hormonal changes, and the aging body cause sexual difficulty, finding solutions can be challenging. In this chapter, we'll talk about the difficulties facing life on this side of the Garden of Eden.

Pregnancy
Even a healthy, happily anticipated pregnancy can interrupt the normal sexual relationship between husband and wife. This is especially true during the first trimester, when nausea and fatigue can make a woman more interested in sleep than sex. During those months, a wise couple might cultivate sexual contact other than intercourse, for instance, cuddling, massage, bubble baths and extended kissing. Fortunately for most couples, intimacy usually returns to normal during the second trimester.

Though pregnancy may interrupt, it rarely ends a healthy sexual relationship. A new baby's arrival may create a more serious problem. Don't forget that your body needs time to heal from the trauma of delivery, whether by cesarean section or vaginal birth.

Most doctors advise their patients to abstain from intercourse for four to six weeks after the baby's birth. This may seem like a long time, however extreme sleep deprivation can make both partners less interested in sex.

By the time your baby sleeps through the night, your body should be completely healed and ready for action. After a baby, continue to cherish the sexual part of your relationship. Though your new baby may consume your attention, remember how important intercourse is to your spouse. In spite of the challenges your new baby brings, resume sexual activity as soon as your doctor declares you fit.

Post-Partum Depression
In rare cases, the hormonal upheaval caused by pregnancy, delivery, and breastfeeding can make it difficult for a woman to get back to her "old" self. **If you find yourself excessively emotional, unable to enjoy everyday activities, having difficulty relating to, or caring for your newborn, or uninterested in caring for yourself, it may be time to bring these concerns to your doctor.** These symptoms may surface within days of childbirth but only become unbearable as a woman begins to contemplate a return to outside employment. No matter how or when your symptoms present, your doctor will be able to help you decide if you suffer from post-partum depression. This illness is easily treatable, even for breastfeeding mothers. You owe it to yourself, your baby and your sex life to seek the help you need to get back to "normal."

Treatment can turn night into day!

Breast Feeding
A large number of women experience decreased interest in sex during breastfeeding. While some experts blame the problem on prolactin, a hormone that is responsible for milk production, it is true that women also experience other troubling changes as well. Lack of sleep, interrupted sleep, and the

exhaustion of newborn care can steal the energy needed for sexual expression.

In addition most breastfeeding women do not ovulate causing estrogen levels to fall. Those changing hormones can leave vaginal tissues with less lubrication, making sex unpleasant or even painful. Full breasts can be sensitive or leaky (causing discomfort or embarrassment) during sex. The striking changes of a post-partum body can leave a woman feeling insecure. All of these issues may influence a woman's ability to enjoy sexual contact after the arrival of a new baby. The good news is that for most of us, these changes go away with time.

I wouldn't advise that a woman stop breastfeeding in order to reclaim her libido. Instead, consider these options: Make rest a priority during the early days following a birth. Nap when your baby naps; it's not just about your body (which is important), but good rest can boost your relationship with your husband. Let go of other responsibilities. I was delighted to discover that my son-in-law had filled the cabinets with paper plates when his first daughter was born. He decided that in those early days washing dishes was an unnecessary chore.

Housework can wait. I promise you that dirt and laundry will not go away. Why hurry? For a season consider disposable diapers and paper napkins. Consider using short-cut meals featuring frozen entrees and pre-made dishes from the deli.

Try breastfeeding just before bed, so that your breasts are empty when you resume sex. Consider vaginal lubricants; many are available over the counter. These may ease the discomfort you feel as you wait for your normal hormone levels to return.

During the early days after the birth of a baby, it is critical to foster husband-wife intimacy. In whatever ways you can, invite your husband into your world. Have evening picnics together on the family room floor. Cultivate affectionate touch and conversations about things other than your newborn. Don't forget that your spouse enjoys a world outside of diapers and feedings. Sleepless nights and frustrating demands will pass; your relationship together will last a lifetime. Even in the midst of a newborn's demands, continue to invest in intimacy.

Time for Reflection

Looking back, how did giving birth change your sexual relationship? Immediately? In the long term?

How did you overcome your difficulties? What advice would you give a new mother in this area?

Thinking about young kids and school aged children, how have you made space for your sex life?

What has been the biggest difficulty?

Make a list of four things you might do to overcome this difficulty.

Birth control
Some couples believe that we should not interfere with God's blessing in the area of children. These couples use no method of birth control, other than what is routinely referred to as the rhythm method. For these couples, the lack of ovulation during pregnancy and nursing may provide an additional layer of confidence, thus enhancing their sexual pleasure. However, as a child is weaned, these parents may experience one additional problem. Without realizing it, the fear of pregnancy may rob these couples of the inherent joy of their sexual relationship. Those who choose to use no birth control must honestly weigh their values against the potential loss of enjoyment in their relationship.

After a new baby, be certain that you and your spouse discuss birth control and the future size of your family. If you want to wait for additional children, what will be your method of birth control? Are you both in agreement? Will you both take responsibility for the plan? For those who believe in birth control, this kind of preparation can give your sexual relationship additional peace and security, allowing you both to relax and enjoy yourselves.

When Birth Control is a Problem
Hormonal birth control has been widely available since the 1960's. What began with "the pill," has expanded to include other delivery systems, such as sub-dermal pellets, the vaginal ring, and the patch. In general, though the delivery system varies, all these work by suppressing the female's normal egg production and release. (Some have other effects. Be sure to check with your doctor.).

While these products contain artificial estrogen, those levels tend to be static throughout the use of the product. In addition most providers prescribe the lowest effective dose for their patients. By simulating pregnancy, these products keeps the ovaries from releasing additional eggs. The lower estrogen levels produced by birth control medications are quite unlike the fluctuating levels (with their peaks and valleys) produced in the normal female reproductive cycle.

By supressing the release of the egg from the ovary, a user experiences no accompanying release of testosterone (which is at least partly responsible for a woman's sex drive). The loss of testosterone may be responsible for some loss of libido in women using hormonal contraception.

All of these factors, taken together, may cause an unwanted depression of a woman's sex drive. If, while using birth control, these side effects begin to diminish her relationship with her spouse, it may be time to consider another birth control product. Perhaps switching dosage, or brand, or changing the delivery system (moving from a daily pill to a vaginal ring, for instance), may restore a woman's normal interest in sex. In some cases, a physician may choose to combine hormones (by adding small amounts of testosterone) to mimic a more normal hormone environment.

If the artificial hormones used in contemporary birth control become problematic (causing an irretrievable loss in sexual interest, or prolonged depression, etc.), it may be time to consider switching to a mechanical/physical method of birth control, such as the diaphragm or the condom.

Depression
Not all depression is linked to childbirth. Sometimes, depression occurs spontaneously, without external crisis or provocation.

This illness may be the biggest threat to a happy and healthy sex life. In fact, it may threaten life in every way. Undiagnosed, depression saps energy, paints the world in dark, monochromatic colors, and makes relationships difficult. The symptoms of depression may be masked by other ongoing issues—a job loss, a move, a difficult marriage, or the loss of a loved one. By this I mean that persistent depression may be blamed on an ongoing difficulty or loss. These very real struggles mask the need for additional support.

However, when normal sleep patterns change, when weight is lost or gained without intention, when interest in favorite activities wanes or disappears altogether, when one feels frequently irritable, when life feels overwhelming or hopeless, it is time to take a close look at your health. It's definitely time to see a doctor.

I am often surprised by Christians who view depression as a failure of their faith. This kind of thinking puts additional and unfair pressure on an already stressed individual. It fails to remember that the human soul is contained within a remarkably frail body. A friend once said to me, "The human body and the human soul live so close together that they catch one another's diseases." Hers is a tremendously insightful statement.

Once, as our church leadership discussed the need for intervention among our members, one of our team said, "There was a time when I was so depressed that it didn't matter who counseled me. I wasn't capable of thinking straight until I was diagnosed and medicated. Then, when I felt like myself again, I didn't need counseling." Her experience completely transformed her understanding of depression and the need for medical intervention. I too have experienced depression.

My doctor, a physician with two medical specialties (at the time he was providing hormonal expertise to the largest fertility clinic in western Washington), told me, "When a woman comes to my office crying, I always assume something is medically wrong. In women especially, tears are often the first indicator that the hormone system is acting up." In his experience medical conditions often first manifest themselves in emotional symptoms. In my case, my thyroid gland had completely stopped working.

Depression occurs in both men and women. I have watched it nearly destroy a friend's marriage. Her husband, a police officer, lived a high-stress, life-on-the-line existence. The endless pressure, the daily life and death adrenaline rush eventually burned out his body's ability to cope. Because he was a man, no one had considered that his withdrawal, his disinterest in his marriage and family might be based in a chemical imbalance.

Instead, he blamed his condition on a bad marriage. His wife was desperate, and considered divorce. Their misery dragged on for years. However, when his doctor finally prescribed medication, his entire personality changed. Their life together, though not perfect, was transformed.

Because depression in men is especially under diagnosed, I encourage women to be vigilant. Should your husband's interest in sex diminish, don't assume that something is wrong with your marriage, or that your husband is having an affair. Instead look for other symptoms of depression. It may be that a heart-to-heart discussion about his health will encourage your husband to see his doctor.

If you find yourself struggling to get out of bed, having difficulty keeping up with every day life, or fighting a sense of lingering disappointment or sadness, ask yourself if it's time to do something. See a doctor. Talk to someone with wisdom and perspective. **Research shows that depressed patients experience the fastest and most complete recovery when both counseling and medications are used. Be open to whatever it takes to reclaim your life. When your body is healthy, your soul can prosper.**

Time for Reflection

How might high or unreasonable life expectations influence a woman? Can you see a connection between high expectations and depression?

List some of these expectations. Of Parenthood?

Of Work?

Of Marriage (or of husbands)?

Of Christianity (or of "Christian" behavior)?

Have you experienced depression? What was your first symptom? Did you seek treatment? Why? Why not? How hard was it to ask for help?

Imagine that you suspect your best friend is struggling with depression. What might you say that would encourage her to seek help? If you are working as a group, can you discuss your approach together?

Hormones and Aging
Over the course of a lifetime, most women thrive in the normal ebb and flow of hormones coursing through their body. After all, from her early teen years through menopause, a woman experiences a fairly regular cycle of hormonal fluctuation. Most wives cope with this normal fluctuation and its associated swings in sexual interest. Later in life things may change.

Peri-Menopause and Menopause
Before modern medicine, women experiencing the many discomforts of "the change" had few options. Serious symptoms often ended active intercourse, leaving couples to find other expressions of sexual intimacy. Some did. Others abandoned physical intimacy all together. I am grateful that modern science has changed much of that.

A woman has reached menopause when she has gone more than twelve months without a period. The ten years before her periods end mark the winding down of a woman's reproductive system. Doctor's call these the perimenopause years.

Women can begin perimenopause at any age; some experience symptoms as early as 35. Others wait until their late 40s. **During this time, a woman may experience irregular periods, changes in her bleeding patterns, weight gain, hot flashes, and vaginal dryness. She may experience constipation and the sudden onset of urinary tract infections.**

While these external signs are noticeable, other, more subtle symptoms may plague her as well. She may have trouble sleeping and difficulty with concentration. She may experience PMS for the first time, or if she has had it before, her symptoms may worsen. She may find herself fighting irritability or even rage.

Some women experience the unexplained onset of depression. Any one of these symptoms may influence a woman's ability to enjoy her sexuality. Taken together, they may combine to destroy her sex life.

At the same time, women in their forties experience other challenges—teenage children, aging parents, escalating job responsibilities. This additional stress can make physical changes even more difficult. When these symptoms begin to feel overwhelming, or unending, or if you spend more time feeling miserable than you do feeling healthy and well, it is time to seek help. At the risk of sounding like a scratched CD, I encourage you to find a physician well-trained in the treatment of perimenopause and menopause. **If your doctor ignores your complaints, or worse, belittles you as being oversensitive or needy, it's time to seek a new treatment provider. A well-trained physician takes these struggles seriously and works to help you through the natural changes your body experiences.**

Hormonal support can help with hot flashes, ease the discomfort of PMS, and restore normal concentration. Creams, tablets, and vaginal rings can deliver estrogen to dry and or irritated vaginal tissues without altering blood estrogen levels (especially helpful for those with estrogen sensitive cancers or cancer risks). These treatments can end repetative urinary tract infections (UTI) as well. Temporary use of antidepressants can ease depression caused by hormonal transition.

Some natural supplements (recommended by a physician) may ease symptoms as well. Remember the FDA does not regulate natural supplements; the ingredients listed on those labels may or may not even be in the supplement, and the quantity and quality of the active ingredients are not subject to government inspection. When you see your doctor, you should probably have your thyroid function, vitamin D levels, blood sugars, and blood lipids checked—all of which may be upset by your changing body.

What's the Point?
The key point is that a wise woman doesn't let these natural changes interfere with her physical or emotional connection with her husband. **We live in a fallen world. We occupy fallen bodies. Occasionally, we need intervention. There is no shame in asking for help.** If finances are difficult, look for low cost or "ability to pay" clinics in your area. You may be able to find referrals to both clinics and doctors via your local hospital, a local woman's shelter, or public health department.

Time for Reflection

Imagine that you have observed your husband retreat sexually. How might you begin a conversation about this?

What is at stake with this kind of conversation? What might he "hear" you say?

(Remember, you must never make an assumption about what is going on in someone else's life. Always ask first!)

Suppose you are struggling with your own interest in sex. Do you feel safe enough to discuss this with your spouse? How might you explain this problem to your husband? When? What message might he hear in your words?

How can you help him hear you more accurately?

Impotence
Not long ago, discussing impotence would have been considered crass and inappropriate. For the most part, there was nothing most men could do about their condition. In general, doctors simply advised their patients to "relax," assuring them that the problem was psychological, and would eventually take care of itself. Recent developments in medical science have changed all that, and most of us are aware of at least one readily available solution—the little blue pill.

Lately, we've been inundated by commercials for drugs developed to assist with erectile dysfunction. They feature youngish men romancing their lovely and equally young partners. The little blue pill has become the brunt of late night television jokes and the source of hundreds of junk emails. But what is erectile dysfunction? What causes it? And what can be done about it?

In order for a normal erection to occur, the male penis must have healthy blood vessels (both arterial supply into the penis and venus outflow), adequate innervation (from the spinal cord and from the brain), and suitable sensory response (to stimulation). If any one of these pieces is missing, the resulting erection may be compromised. For this reason, when difficulty arises, a man should be screened for multiple physical conditions. Don't give in to the anonymous ease of purchasing questionable Internet drugs.

Chronic diseases can affect male sexual function. Nervous system diseases, like Multiple Sclerosis, or Parkinsonism may cause difficulty. Diseases of the hormone system, such as thyroid disease, diabetes, or prostate changes may affect sexual function. And of course, vascular changes can cause significant trouble.

As a man ages, the vascular changes he experiences affect all the vessels of his body. The tiny arteries in his heart may be clogged, leading to heart disease. The vessels in his limbs may be compromised, leading to peripheral vascular disease (and sensory-motor changes in the feet and legs). These conditions are believed to be related to elevated blood pressure and blood lipid levels experienced by some aging adults. Because those changes are happening everywhere in the body, they may also occur in the vasculature of the penis.

For this reason many cardiologists begin their new patient interviews by asking, "So, how's your sex life?" In the world of peripheral vasculature, significant changes often show up first in the penis. These patients may complain of difficulty obtaining or maintaining an erection. On further exam, cardiologists often find changes in the cardiac vessels at well. It is as if the sexual function of the penis is a window into the health of the body.

Not all erectile dysfunction indicates cardiac compromise. Drug, tobacco and alcohol use, prostate surgery, depression (and other psychological conditions), some medicines, falling testosterone levels, spinal cord injury or degeneration, severe obesity and even prolonged stress can cause erectile dysfunction. Only a trained medical professional can tease out the potential cause and treatments available. Please don't even think about purchasing medication from an email. The risk is that while you seek to treat sexual dysfunction, you ignore the deadly threat of diabetes or serious, even fatal heart disease.

Women should be aware that normal aging causes changes in most men. When stimulated, the aging penis may become less rigid than in younger years. In order to maintain an erection, the older male may need repeated stimulation. These changes are normal. Though they can be troublesome, they are manageable in the context of a loving relationship.

If erectile dysfunction continues despite making healthy lifestyle changes, it may be time to see a doctor. With careful questions, he can zero in on the problem. Because this difficulty may be embarrassing for your spouse, your gentle encouragement may give him the courage to visit his doctor. Restoring your sexual relationship is well worth the effort.

Cancer
This diagnosis and its accompanying worries can completely obliterate any concern for sexual health. The type of cancer you (as a couple) face—whether breast cancer, blood cancer, prostate cancer, or lung cancer—makes little difference. For both partners, the first and primary issue becomes survival. "How will we treat this?" patients ask, followed closely by, "Will I survive?"

The significance of the diagnosis so overwhelms every other area of life that the issue of sexual intimacy becomes a moot point. Treatment may begin with traumatic surgery, followed by a long and sometimes complicated recovery. This is often followed eventually by chemotherapy, and perhaps radiation. Medical procedures and treatments may span months or even years. Patients often lose weight, energy, concentration and focus. Sometimes, they even lose interest in life.

The patient's spouse (the healthy partner), continues his professional life as he struggles to keep the household running, caring for children, for the cancer patient, managing the drug schedule, the doctor appointments, and the caring attention of so many friends. Before long, both the patient and his caregiver are exhausted and overwhelmed. Sex is the last thing on anyone's mind.

Even doctors, focused as they are on the cancer battle, are reluctant to address this significant loss of sexual intimacy.

When survival becomes recovery and recovery becomes cure, a husband and wife begin the search to recover their lost love life. It may not be easy. **Many chemotherapy regimens effectively kick young women into menopause. This sudden and unexpected result of cancer treatment can have serious consequences on your love life.** At the same time, the cancer diagnosis itself may limit your problem-solving options.

If a woman's cancer cells are stimulated by her hormones (what some refer to as hormone positive), her doctor may recommend a hysterectomy (the surgical removal of her ovaries and her uterus). The doctor may follow this with medication designed to block the production or absorption of estrogen anywhere in the body. For her survival those remaining cancer cells must never receive hormonal stimulation.

After this kind of treatment, she faces a lifetime without any real potential for hormone support. Her hormonal environment and thus her emotional and physical world may suddenly change, altering her breast tissue, sex-drive, vaginal lubrication, body shape, bone density, skin, and even her metabolism.

Coping with these changes without the option of hormonal support severely limits available treatment options. Though the couple has survived the trauma of cancer, they may face the loss of normal sexual function. Sometimes, they face that loss without the support of the medical community. I have heard breast cancer survivors seeking sexual help report that their doctors say, "Look, you're alive. Don't worry about the small stuff."

Sexual Intimacy Isn't Small Stuff
When life settles back into a normal routine, you and your spouse will want to resume your sexual relationship. If you need continued support and your own doctor seems less than helpful, consider consulting with a naturopath recommended by, or associated with a large medical-cancer center. These professionals may be able to find natural, safe products that will help you enjoy your sexuality in a pain free way. Their training and experience with cancer survivors will arm them with answers to many common difficulties.

A well trained naturopath will be able to deal with issues of lubrication, allergies, condom use, and may even be able to give a natural boost to your libido. Another resource may be a consultation with an endocrinologist or OB-GYN who specializes in hormonal issues. You may find this kind of expert at a local fertility clinic. Because they treat many women who have survived breast and reproductive cancers, they may have exactly the information or referral you need.

While things may never be exactly as they were before your diagnosis, don't settle for abandoning your sexual relationship. If you cannot resolve the physical problems, even with professional medical help, consider visiting a sex therapist. A therapist who specializes in cancer survivors may be able to give you new direction and new support as you renew your sexual intimacy.

Prostate Cancer
Today, much controversy surrounds the diagnosis and treatment of prostate cancer. Not long ago, a simple blood test, followed by a radical prostatectomy was the only available option for men

facing this diagnosis. Today, from diagnosis to treatment, science has radically changed the face of prostate cancer.

Today, cryotherapy, nuclear seed placement, conventional radiation, proton beam therapy, robotic surgery, traditional surgery, hormone therapy, and active monitoring are all used in the battle against this common, but not often deadly disease. (Though one in six men will be diagnosed with prostate cancer in their lifetime, according to the American Cancer Society, only one in 35 men who are diagnosed will actually die of the disease.).

The basic problem, which connects prostate cancer to sexual function, lies in the secrets of human anatomy. The walnut-sized prostate gland, which lies at the base of the penis, directly below the bladder, is encased in a tiny network of nerves and blood vessels, which provide stimulation and blood flow to the penis.

As doctors destroy the cancer cells inside the prostate, treatments frequently damage these tiny, fragile nerves and vessels surrounding the gland itself, leaving the patient unable to function sexually. Most often the damage repairs itself. However when it does not, the patient experiences impotence.

The treatment of prostate related sexual dysfunction is beyond the scope of this project. However, the American Cancer Society websiste, located at www.cancer.org, is rich with resources for the prostate cancer survivor and suggests discussion topics for you and your doctor.

All of us should be aware of some basic information: Current research suggests that stimulating the penis immediately after prostate cancer treatment yields better long-term recovery for a sexually functional erection. However, if normal function does not return, hope is not lost. In fact, there are a great many available options.

First, your doctor will want to measure nighttime erection activity with an electronic monitor. This tells him whether or not the penis is physically able to initiate an erection. With tiny bands attached to the penis, the doctor can measure the size and rigidity of a nighttime erection.

An ultrasound exam can determine the amount and direction of blood flow to the penis. Nerve tests reveal the sensitivity of the skin. Blood tests check for blood levels of testosterone and prolactin. Taken together, this information gives a clearer picture of the source of post-surgical erectile dysfunction and suggests the best course of treatment.

Surviving prostate cancer isn't enough. When at all possible, both husband and wife should seek additional help to recover their sexual intimacy. It is one of the foundation stones of your relationship. Doctors can help, but only if you discuss this deeply personal complication of treatment.

Time for Reflection

When someone you love faces a cancer diagnosis, how do you offer support?

Thinking about the importance of sexual intimacy, how might you support this need for your cancer-patient friend?

Would you feel comfortable asking someone about their intimacy during or after cancer treatment? Why? Why not?
How might the fear of impotence influence a man's willingness to test for, or seek treatment for symptoms of prostate cancer?

Armed With Information
Most prostate cancer is found during a routine physical. For that reason, regular medical check ups may actually save a man's life. Sometimes, when a man hasn't been seen regularly, prostate cancer has enough time to cause physical signs. In general, those signs are created by the presence of an enlarged prostate gland, which impedes the passage of urine and or semen along the urethra. These signs, which do not by themselves confirm a cancer diagnosis, should be followed up by a doctor as soon as possible:

- Blood in the semen or urine
- Difficulty urinating while standing
- Pain during ejaculation or urination
- Weak or interupted stream during urination
- Leakage of urine while coughing, or laughing
- Increased urinary frequency (needing to go to the bathroom) espcially at night

Obesity
Regardless of the cause, obesity markedly affects human sexuality. In a 2008 study published in the *Journal of Sexual Medicine*, Italian doctors studied more than 2,500 male patients who sought treatment for sexual dysfunction. Nearly 60% of those patients were overweight or obese. In the study, doctors found a clear correlation between serum testosterone levels and obesity. The more severe the obesity, the lower the blood testosterone levels.

Another strong correlation was found between obesity, high blood pressure, and abnormal penile blood flow. The study authors suggest that high blood pressure damages the small vessels of the penis. **These important links seem to indicate that for men, obesity clearly causes physical changes that impair the normal function of the penis. If for no other reason, men should be encouraged to make better lifestyle choices with the goal of maintaining their sexual health.** Cutting back on calories and increasing exercise might give men a longer healthier sex life. A wise wife can help her husband make these changes.

For women, the effects of obesity on sexual health seem less physically based. A study published in the journal *Obesity*, (Volume 14, #3) reviewed the sexual function of more than 1000 overweight participants. Of the women in the study, about 1/3 reported that they usually or always did not enjoy sexual activity, had little sexual desire, experienced difficulty with performance, and avoided sexual encounters. About half of the obese women reported difficulty in these areas some of the time.

Men, however, had other concerns. About half of the overweight men reported difficulty with performance at least some of the time. Just over 40% reported lack of sexual desire at least some of the time. **In both men and women, the higher the BMI (an indication of obesity) the more likely the participant was to have sexual difficulty.**

In the United States, about 37% of people are obese. That rate is expected to go up in the next ten years. Some experts estimate that within fifty years half the population will qualify as obese. Due to this growing health problem, physicians and scientists have now added new categories to describe these previously unseen levels of obesity.

A BMI (Body Mass Index) of 25-29.9 is considered "overweight." "Obese" describes those with BMI over 30. "Morbidly obese" describes patients with BMI from 40-50 and "Super Obese" describes those with BMI measurements over 50. (You can easily discover your own BMI by using one of the many calculators now available on the web).

Many factors play into the development of obesity: metabolism, genetics, activity level, endocrine function, ethnicity, culture, dietary habits, socioeconomic status, smoking, pregnancy, menopause, psychology, diabetes. While many of these issues cannot be changed, some can.

Maintaining a healthy body weight is good for your health, for your heart, for your life. It helps you to avoid metabolic disease, heart disease, diabetes, high blood pressure, and many kinds of cancer. However, maintaining a normal body weight increases the chances that you will enjoy sex longer and more fully than your overweight peers.

If avoiding illness isn't enough motivation, perhaps sexual fulfillment will be. **If your spouse has difficulty with poor eating habits, begin to cook mindfully. Restrict the unhealthy foods that you bring into your home, focusing on those with high nutritional payback for the calorie count.** Cut out high calorie deserts, substituting fruit instead. Keep a fruit bowl on your kitchen counter. Empty your cookie jar and put it away.

A small but healthy change begins by simply including a vegetable with every meal. Encourage your spouse to join you for walks after dinner and on the weekends (even if you've already finished your exercise for the day). Remember that no exercise program will continue unless you enjoy it. Look for physical activites you can enjoy together, like hiking, skiing, tennis, running, walking, horseback riding, and kyaking.

While you cannot control your husband's choices, you can make it easier for him (and for you) to choose the best options available. You can live as an inspiration, taking good care of your body, your health and your weight.

I know one couple who made a healthier lifestyle their common goal. Together they lost more than one hundred pounds, conquering the downward pull of inactivity and poor diet. These days, they enjoy both physical activity and healthy eating. You can do it too. Consider it a major investment in your sex life!

Time for Reflection

Thinking about your family, imagine that your husband has begun to put on weight. You worry that this might affect his health. How might you begin a conversation without causing hurt feelings?

What changes might your family make that would help him decrease his daily calorie count?

How might you increase fiber in your husband's daily diet?

What "swaps" might you make in routine foods? Where might you find healthy recipies for evening meals?

What might you do to encourage your husband to increase his activity level?

Worth the Work
Over the course of your lives together you will likely encounter many obstacles to a healthy sex life. Many of these, like pregnancy, menopause and occasional illness, are completely normal. Most interuptions are temporary. Though these and other more severe challenges may change the *way* you enjoy sex together, with support and determination, none of these physical challenges should end your expressions of intimacy. Together, you and your spouse can maintain a great sexual relationship for a lifetime.

CHAPTER

Going the Distance

Sometimes, life feels like a marathon. Sometimes, marriage feels longer.

In the beginning you are fresh and full of confidence. You believe you've found the best partner on the planet. Though you expect to experience difficulty, you believe your love is strong enough to overcome every obstacle. On your wedding day, it never occurs to you that your own spouse may become the very obstacle you must overcome.

This chapter is about that kind of obstacle—the kind brought on by your spouse. Not cancer, or financial hardship, not physical illness or natural disaster. This chapter is about a tornado your spouse brings home when he embraces infidelity, addiction, violence, or pornography. It is also about the supernatural strength that only the Holy Spirit can bring to your marriage.

This chapter is about God's ability to give warning, advice, and wisdom when you most need it. It is about His ability to heal and salve the broken heart. It is about His ability to provide the power to forgive—even when you have no strength for such a herculean task.

If you listen to Oprah, you will hear that a violent man can never change. Dr. Phil will tell you that an unfaithful man can never be trusted. If you believe Anderson Cooper, you will believe that a homosexual cannot repent and turn from sin. **In fact, not only do most of today's cultural *prophets* deny the possibility for change, for the most part they also deny the *need* for change.**

You are what you are, they declare, and that is all you need ever be. This is not biblical truth. The Bible tells us that all humans come to God in our most wretched state. Sinful, unable to help ourselves, hopeless, we experience the supernatural cleansing found only in Jesus Christ. His sacrifice makes our salvation possible. **We enter into Christ as smelly, hopeless and chained as a street-bound drug addict. But Jesus does not leave us there.**

Instead, He breaks the chains that hold us to our past. And in the process, He promises transformation. In place of our shattered past, He gives us an utterly new life. This is our heritage in Christ. We are not simply saved. We are changed. We are not just changed at salvation; God gives us His power to continue that transformation—from faith to deeper faith—for a lifetime.

In every interaction, in every difficulty, in every struggle, the Holy Spirit seeks to make us less like our old self and more like Jesus. It is a difficult walk. Sometimes it is frightening. Sometimes the difficulty makes us sweat. For this journey we must lace up our boots, pick up our pack, and climb the high road He has set before us. For some, Jesus seems to choose an even higher, steeper path. For those pilgrims, the rocks are loose, and the edge falls from dizzying heights.

These are the stories of couples who have chosen to walk the higher path. Some include the actual names of the persons involved. They have chosen to reveal their stories publically. Others use pseudonyms to protect the innocent. In sharing these stories, I do not mean to play the game "beat my pain." Please don't compare your difficulty to the trouble which these women experienced. By doing so, you may exclude yourself from hope.

The fact is God can do anything with and through anyone. As the scriptures say, "With God, all things are possible."

Nancy and Bob

I met Nancy through a mutual friend. With supernatural grace, she has allowed me to include her story, which is here excerpted from her own keynote address given to hurting women. (Betrayal Redeemed: A Journey from Hurt to Hope, October 13, 2012, Lake Oswego Oregon (by www.tuffstuffministries.com). With Nancy's permission, I have shortened her story in order contain it here:

On June 6, 2000, Nancy's first marriage ended. On that day her husband Bob called her at work and asked her to come home immediately. Once home, he confessed that he had contracted genital herpes from a "one-week" affair with a woman he had met via the Internet.

What Bob began as a simple confession evolved into an almost endless discovery of a lifetime of lies and betrayals. In spite of abundant physical evidence, Bob resisted telling Nancy the whole truth about his secret life. In the months after his initial confession, as she pressed for details, Nancy caught Bob in lie after lie. Eventually, armed with his visa and phone bills, access to his email passwords and accounts, Nancy knew enough.

Bob had been involved with a series of women over the course of their entire twenty-three year marriage. Though the marriage had its difficulties, Nancy had no idea her husband had been unfaithful. He led worship at the church where she taught Sunday school. What trouble they experienced, she blamed on her own inadequacies. Though he frequently traveled for work, Nancy had no idea that Bob also trolled for women online, and then traveled to meet them for sex. She did not know that his affair with a woman in their own church had destroyed the woman's marriage. Nancy had no idea that her husband had become a sex-addict.

Her world collapsed. Nancy said, "Through this early period of our "recovery" (could I really even call it recovery yet?) I felt like I was going crazy. I had trouble making simple decisions—like what to have for dinner. What to wear. How to answer questions. All my houseplants died. I sat at work and stared out the window, rehearsing old conversations. Ruminating—like chewing the cud—over and over. Re-thinking memories of times before disclosure that he had done or said something odd—trying to figure out if they pointed to other affairs. For a while I honestly believed my husband (who was he, anyway?) was going to kill me.

"During that time, we went to Crater Lake for a mini-vacation, and I refused to let him stand behind me. I became hyper-vigilant, dreamed about "catching" him—horrible vivid dreams of him with his mistresses. I quit eating—which is a sign of depression for me, and lost 30 pounds in 2 months. His lying—and finding the truth—[became] my obsession. There was no trust. No happiness. No parenting. We were just in survival-mode and I didn't think I could make it."

During those initial months, Nancy realized that Bob lacked repentance. "So I asked him to leave. I think at that time I finally realized that by allowing him to stay in our home, I was keeping him from 'hitting bottom.' After he moved out, he eventually admitted to over 20 years of sexual acting out—visiting prostitutes, viewing porn, and going to strip clubs . . . And when he discovered how easy it was to meet women in online chat rooms who were willing to meet him for sex, he stopped using prostitutes, and spent hours cruising on-line and then traveling [to where his victims were]." Though his infidelity never left her thoughts, at least with him out of the house, Nancy no longer spent her time yelling at Bob.

Bob did hit bottom. He began seeing a counselor. He joined two different recovery support groups. Both Bob and Nancy read books. Though Bob resisted being labeled as a sex addict (he felt that any man would behave as he had), something changed after reading Ted Robert's book, *Pure Desire*. At last, Bob reluctanctly admitted, "I have some of the characteristics of a sex addict."

As a couple, they experienced the cruel rejection of some in the church. For almost two years, her senior pastor refused to speak to Nancy. "And believe it or not, being shunned wasn't the worst reaction. Some people—men and women—actually said that this must have been my fault. These weren't just wackos—these were my Christian friends! They insisted that if I had been sexier, or more loving or more exciting, my husband wouldn't have needed to look outside our relationship for love."

Nancy also experienced the loving support of deep friendship. "I also had some wonderful responses from dear friends—in the church and out—who not only embraced me, but who also stood beside Bob and remained his friend, not judging him, but also not approving of his actions. He was so overwhelmed with the shame of his behavior—actually we both were—that we needed this kind of acceptance and love.

"We were very sick and it was like medicine. I really appreciated the people who could hear our confession and still treat us like they had before—truly nonjudgmental. One of those dear women ministered to us in a truly a merciful and compassionate way for several years. She would listen for hours while we walked or sat and I cried or ranted or raged. The first meal I ate after Bob's disclosure was at her house—I guess I felt safe there—3 weeks after he told me."

On September 11, 2001, Bob and Nancy joined the rest of the nation watching the destruction of the World Trade Center towers in New York City. Nancy describes their conversation this way:

"That evening, Bob said to me, 'What happened today is kind of like what I did to you. Just out of nowhere, I destroyed your life.' He was starting to get it.

"And he was right. After the devastation, destruction and denial that Bob had bombed our marriage with, I had lots of rubble to sort through. What about our marriage was real? Who was he, really? What memories did I need to re-think? What might a new marriage with this man look like? Could we even stay married? I quit wearing my wedding ring—that marriage had ended on June 6, 2000. I wasn't sure it could ever be repaired and for sure, I couldn't rebuild on the rubble of lies and deceit. Before a foundation for our marriage could be started, we needed to do some heavy work first clearing the rubble."

During the next two years, Nancy joined a support group. Long after the original disclosure, Nancy was astounded to discover how easily Bob lied to her. Once, in a support meeting, she expressed her longing for her old life. Her group leader laughed. She told Nancy that what she missed was the beautiful lie. **"It's much better to know the ugly truth than the beautiful lie," her leader said. "And better to know the man as he really is than what he pretended to be."**

With much professional help, Nancy worked toward rebuilding trust. In the process, she also discovered that she suffered from Post-traumatic Stress Disorder. Her forgiveness, she says, was a process, interrupted by frequent bouts of trauma.

She describes it in her own words. "I began to realize that forgiveness was a constant, on-going reaction to the reminders of his adultery. And so many things were reminders . . . church, worship music (which was healing to Bob, triggered anger and memory to me), pictures of him—including pictures of our family—so I put all the pictures in my house under the bed. For years.

"Other reminders were any affection or sex, any music, any traveling—motels were a huge trigger for me, any alcohol—I don't drink, but Bob would drink when he was acting out—even just catching sight of him—that man that I used to think was so wonderful and handsome—and my brain would start to roil and ruminate. Circular thoughts that were awful—depressing, sad, angry. This wasn't me!

"**Forgiveness is a process that happens when it happens and no one can tell you how long it takes or when it (the offense) will stop popping up and surprising you with its intensity**. It's been 12 years since his last adultery and nine years since his last intentional lie (I think), yet I still get these emotional responses. The PTSD (Post Traumatic Stress Disorder) part of the shock is learning that your life and your marriage isn't what you thought it was, and it's out of your control."

In the 12 years since Bob confessed his infidelity, both Bob and Nancy have struggled to clear away the rubble and build a new relationship. Gone is Bob's guilt. Gone too are Nancy's frantic efforts to fix herself and her marriage. Gone are the false expectations and her naiveté.

Nancy is a survivor. She is wiser, beloved of God, a forgiver. She is not a fool. "Unfortunately, I still am aware that Bob has the capability of lying to me and cheating on me. I carry the phone number of a divorce lawyer in my purse at all times and I have pre-decided that I will ask him to leave immediately if he betrays me. I have vowed to myself that I will not go through this again and I intend to keep my vow. My husband still travels for business, but I insist that he answer every call he receives from me and does not ever travel over weekends. My first response to anything out of the ordinary is to question his motives and his honesty. This makes him very sad, but this is the marriage he created by his actions. I am not unhappy.

"My children love their dad and respect him, we have grandchildren we enjoy together, and we are creating relationships in a new church that isn't the church of my upbringing or the church of our healing. It is a place that understands sin and grace and redemption. The people in this church don't judge people by their pasts."

Bob and Nancy have a new marriage, a second marriage, one characterized by both forgiveness and wisdom. They have survived. And, they have vowed to share their story and the hope of God's grace with anyone who will listen. "The fact that Bob was willing to give up his secret life and go through the work of confession and counseling for all those years—that willingness was from God. Bob had prayed that God would give him a contrite heart and create a clean spirit within him and God answered abundantly. And the ability and desire I had to forgive Bob was also from God. None of this is from our own abilities. It's all because of Him and His grace to us."

Connie and Roger

Looking at Connie and Roger today, you would never suspect the dark past they have survived together.

Quiet and soft-spoken, Roger meticulously maintains his beautiful yard and home. Connie prefers people and lively conversations to housework and cooking. Today, both Connie and Roger have a deep desire to heal hurting hearts. Having been wounded themselves, they come to that passion honestly.

Almost forty-one years ago, Connie worked as a congressional secretary in central California. Roger served in the United States Navy in Hawaii. They found one another through Roger's sister, (who was Connie's friend) and grew their friendship via a continual flow of letters. Roger managed to make trips to California when he could. Connie flew back and forth as well. Between May and the following March their friendship grew into love. Eventually they married.

In Honolulu, the bride and groom enjoyed friendships with others from Santa Rosa. Connie found work as a preschool teacher. Their relationship with their church grew. Because money was scarce, they found ingenious ways to entertain themselves. Along with another couple, Roger and Connie created furniture from the Navy shipyard's discarded pine.

In those early days, Connie noticed odd things about Roger. He was embarrassed to hold her hand or put an arm around her in public. Though disappointed, she dismissed this as part of his personality. Gradually, she became aware of Roger's temper as it flared in unexpected and frightening ways. "I remember it happening when he was working on a car, and something went wrong," Connie told me. "I grew up in a home without any boys. Though I'd dated a lot, I thought to myself, maybe this is just the way men are. Maybe all men are quick tempered. I didn't know any better." She began to avoid provoking his anger.

Gradually Roger's anger grew more problematic; Connie's fear grew as well. Then, unexpectedly, he was sent away for an eight-month deployment. While he was gone, Connie began to wonder if she'd made a mistake in marrying the sailor from New Mexico. When he returned from sea, his anger pattern escalated. "He cycled through these predictable phases about every month," Connie said. "I was so ashamed of what was happening, I didn't tell anyone. No one talked about domestic violence in those days. I was so alone."

Years went by before Connie and Roger sought help from their church. One day, in their pastor's office, Roger and Connie were asked to kneel and pray on opposite sides of the room. "We were supposed to just listen to the Holy Spirit. I did that, and I had the strongest sense that Roger really did want to change. That gave me the courage to move forward." But courage wasn't enough to end his rage.

Eventually, the couple and their two young children returned to Southern California. They sought counseling, but discovered how difficult it was to find someone who understood domestic violence. Roger seemed trapped in a cycle he could not break. Connie, weary and discouraged, resigned herself to ending the marriage. About that time Roger's company asked him to relocate to the Pacific Northwest. At first, Connie refused to move. It seemed the logical time to separate. But a Focus on the Family radio broadcast changed the course of their marriage.

Connie told me, "It was a program about Domestic Violence, about a pastor whose rage had destroyed his family and his ministry. Somehow, he managed to turn his life around. It was the first time I'd ever heard that this unbelievable horror I was living in could be changed. I saw a glimmer of hope for the first time."

Roger scouted the Pacific Northwest, looking for a counselor. Connie agreed to give the relationship one more year and move to Washington only under the condition that their home in California sold immediately. The house sold in one day!

In Puyallup, Washington, Roger and Connie bought a home. They began doing recovery work at Northwest Family Life, a counseling group specializing in Domestic Violence. They both gave the program everything they had. Connie attended group counseling twice a week along with other wives. Roger did an identical program at night. It cost money, took enormous energy, and was fraught with setbacks and frustration. They worked in individual counseling. Occasionally, they counseled together.

Eventually, Roger began to understand his anger. He found other, healthier ways to deal with his emotions. His patterns changed.

Connie told me, "In class they told us to remember, 'You didn't cause this problem. You can't cure this problem. You can't control this problem. But you might contribute to it. Your job is to understand how you contribute to his issues.' " It was hard work for both Connie and Roger. There were days when old patterns reemerged for both of them.

It was during those setbacks that Connie needed the most support. She found comfort in a small prayer group from her church. There, Connie could be honest about her marriage without suffering shame or ridicule or endless advice. Their recovery work continued.

"The rage ended fairly quickly after we started our program," Connie told me. "But learning new communication patterns took much longer." Though they were separated for several short periods, as they worked on their behaviors, eventually their relationship began to take new shape. Today, they are a different couple.

"We have a peace together that is gratifying. He gets me now," Connie explains. "We love staying at home, enjoying our friends and our grown children and our four grandsons. We've watched our two grown children recover and heal from the trauma of their childhood. They've had their own journey though this; but God has done a really great work in both of them. I can't wait to see how it all ends up."

Roger and Connie have experienced more challenges than most. During their recovery, a fire destroyed most of their home. Connie has survived two seperate bouts of breast cancer and reconstructive surgery. Roger now lives with a debilitating, life threatening illness. But without their remarkable healing, they would be facing those life challenges alone. Today, they are strong for one another. They have grown as individuals and as a couple. They help others who have no hope. The believe in change because they have experienced it.

Judy and Tom

Not every difficult marriage involves infidelity, pornography, or domestic violence. Sometimes, difficulty simply evolves. It can come from a trying work situation, or difficult relatives. It can develop when a couple faces the challenges of a disabled child, or when one suffers a disabling injury or physical challenge. What happens then?

Judy and Tom discovered that left untended, water isn't the only thing that runs downhill. Hard to imagine that anything could go wrong for a couple who spent their first night together at the Bluebird of Happiness Hotel.

Mid-western native Judy explained, "We were headed to Chicago, but Tom hadn't gotten a reservation for our first night together. All along the interstate hotels were full; then we hit the Bluebird. The lady who managed the place was incredibly excited about our honeymoon. When she showed us the room I couldn't believe it. The floor was covered by carpet samples that had been stitched together by hand, and the sheets were so worn you could read a newspaper through them."

Judy and Tom, who met at church camp, dated a full ten months before tying the knot. After their honeymoon, Tom returned to college and Judy dropped out of school to support the new family. While he finished school, he preached every weekend at tiny country churches. After graduation, he took a job as a youth pastor. Over the next decade, as their family grew, Tom took a succession of pastorates.

Tom was so busy taking care of others, preparing to preach, and growing his congregation that he spent little time with his wife. Resources were limited, and Tom managed money by giving Judy a weekly allowance. "It didn't matter what the kids needed. I had to figure out how to get everything—groceries, clothes, household expenses—out of that weekly allowance. He wouldn't bend."

Tom's control contributed to her resentment. "My parents had a contentious relationship and I was determined not to let that happen. All I'd ever wanted was to be a wife and a mother, but this marriage wasn't turning out the way I'd hoped.

"Being a pastor's wife demanded a lot of confidentiality. I couldn't talk to anyone about what might be going on at home—not to anyone from church, not to anyone from the community." Judy had no one to help her process her frustration.

The tension between Tom and Judy grew. Eventually, he took a job with a large corporation. The new job was unlike anything Tom had ever done before, requiring that he work 60 or 70-hour weeks. His boss was demanding and extremely difficult. When the children entered high school, Judy took a job outside her home. "I don't want to paint a picture that we were always unhappy. We weren't. We had good times. Good memories. But the worst was yet to come."

After the two oldest children left for college, Tom began acting erratically. His emotions waxed and waned. He was tired. Irritable. Explosive. His relationship with his grown children suffered. Judy frequently found herself in the middle of battles between Tom and the children. Fortunately, Tom's doctor diagnosed the beginning of Type II Diabetes.

"That explained the emotional volatility. But by then we'd developed a pattern. We'd drifted apart, coexisting in the same space, but not connected to one another. It wasn't good. We no longer had anything in common."

Some of Judy's friends suggested divorce. In Judy's mind, divorce wasn't an option. When her youngest graduated from high school, it occurred to her that she might have to live 30 or 40 more years with Tom. She began to pray about her options. "I didn't want a divorce. But I didn't want this marriage either. I told my friends that I had one last thing I wanted to try."

Judy decided to become her husband's friend. "I did all the things people do in the beginning. I left notes on his pillow. I made special foods for him. I bought tickets to shows and invited him to join me." Things didn't change all at once. In fact, change was so slow in coming that Judy fought the temptation to give up.

To make matters worse, Tom discovered his corporate job had been given to someone else, and his pay had been cut in half. Judy encouraged him to find new work. He took a job in Massachusetts and they moved. "Though it sounded scary, it turned out to be the best thing that ever happened to us. We didn't know anyone in Massachusetts. We only had one another."

Gradually, Tom began to respond to Judy's overtures. "It wasn't an instant transformation, but eventually Tom began to give back." He returned her affection. Their conversation began to take on a new tone. We began to talk about things we hadn't in years."

Though they did not know it at the time, they did not have long. "We had a wonderful fifteen year period after we left Massachusetts," Judy said. Then Tom was diagnosed with prostate cancer. "The last ten years of Tom's life were completely given to fighting his illness. It wasn't easy for either of us."

Those who knew Tom and Judy during those later years would say that Tom adored his wife. You could see it in the way he watched her, and hear it in the way he spoke about her. **With a smile, Tom used to say "I think people are nice to me just so they can be friends with Judy."**

"I don't want to suggest that what I did might work for everyone," Judy explained. "It certainly won't cure infidelity or violence. But we weren't in that category. We'd simply drifted apart. One of us needed to take the first step back. I decided to be the one." In Judy and Tom's marriage, true healing began when one lonely wife decided to become her husband's friend.

Debbie and Brad

Most couples know very little about one another during their dating days. What they don't know, what they may not even think about, is that when you marry someone, you marry more than a person. You marry their past—both the past they remember and the past they do not.

Debbie met Brad at work. "I wasn't attracted to him at the time; we were both dating other people. But over the months, we saw each other often. I even tried to set him up with some of my friends." Eventually Brad asked Debbie out, and after eighteen months of dating, they married.

Their marriage had happy moments. But these were interrupted by events Debbie describes as just plain bizarre. "As I remember it, the weirdness centered around touch. If I surprised him by sitting too close, or touching him when he didn't expect it, he would pull away. It was such a severe reaction, I just didn't understand."

"Sex was always on Brad's timetable. I couldn't initiate," Debbie said. "It made any intimacy, both physical and emotional, a hit and miss event." They struggled through the arrival of three young children.

Brad was a hard worker and a great provider. Then, after a Christmas shopping trip, Debbie came home to find Brad curled up in a ball under his office desk. "We didn't know what to do; we didn't even call the doctor. I managed to get a babysitter and take him off to a hotel. He slept through the whole weekend, and went back to work on Monday." Brad had suffered a breakdown.

He struggled with caffeine addiction. "Brad didn't just drink a lot of coffee. He drank quarts of coffee. That much caffeine gave him excruciating migraines. It took years for him to decide to stop drinking caffeine."

Brad also drank alcohol. "I didn't know how much he was drinking because he hid it from me." Though things weren't terrible at home, Debbie suspected there was something more. She suspected that Brad was having an affair. "With three little kids, there wasn't much I could do. Thirty years ago, I didn't have any way to substantiate what was happening. I just had to watch and wait." Debbie also prayed.

It didn't take long for the truth to come out. **Brad was involved with a woman from their church. Debbie went to her pastor. "He wanted to sweep the whole thing under the rug. He told me not to talk to anyone about it."** In deep pain and severe shock, Debbie wanted her church's support. Instead, she was told, "I'll call you next week and see how you are doing."

Debbie had no one to talk to, no one to give her advice. She felt abandoned by her church. No one would even talk to her about what had happened. "The only thing I knew for sure was that God wanted me to stay married. I just had this mandate from God. I had no tools, no resources. You wouldn't tell someone who was bleeding to death, 'I can see you in three weeks.'"

Her despair deepened when Brad announced that the woman involved had become pregnant. "Now, suddenly we had a child to protect," Debbie said. She didn't know where to turn. Though they left the church, they continued to limp along.

In the early hours one night, Debbie got a phone call from Brad. He had gone drinking and was stuck in some sleazy part of a nearby city. Refusing to wake the children to go get him, Debbie called one of Brad's friends. Only then did she begin to realize the extent of her husband's drinking problem. Brad began immediate treatment for his alcoholism. Debbie sought counsel for herself, but couldn't seem to find the right fit.

Through a long series of connections, they finally discovered the help they needed. It was in the counselor's office that Brad remembered that he had been sexually abused throughout his childhood. The memories had been there all along, just out of reach. But with the memories, came other truths.

Brad had been drinking since he was in the fourth grade. His mother struggled with mental illness. His father had pornography on the coffee table at home. When Brad was young, his father had an affair and his parents divorced. While any one of these things would be difficult for a child, all of them together proved too much for Brad. His acting out, his drinking, his caffeine addiction—all of these behaviors were part of his way of dealing with the brokenness in his life.

"Each of these issues was like a spore that infected the fruit on the tree of our marriage. And here we were, facing a tree full of really bad fruit." It wasn't easy. Brad and Debbie went to counseling, and read books. Brad joined an accountability group.

Throughout those years, they protected their children. "We saw how much damage these adult issues brought into Brad's life. We made the choice that we wouldn't do that to our kids. We only talked about these issues after the kids were in bed. We did counseling when they were at school. We only told them about the alcoholism when they were old enough to handle it." Brad and Debbie wanted their children to deal with children's issues. "That was a time in their life when their only worry should be whether or not they picked up their blocks."

Today, Brad and Debbie share a deep love. Their grown children are stable, with healthy relationships of their own. Brad has chosen to abstain from alcohol. They do not keep it in their home. "We are so aware of the consequences of our choices. We make very deliberate decisions about our lives." Brad has learned to face his issues. He lives an open life. Though he doesn't approve of his parent's choices, he maintains a relationship with them. He can talk to his children about his past. He has offered relationship to the child from the affair.

Debbie says, "Our relationship today is real. We talk about real things. We are in touch with our true selves. We have new friends, a healthier church, a more supportive pastor. I trust Brad. I am safe with him," Debbie says. "I know that God helped me over this mountain. The path on the other side is easier. God was faithful to walk along side me, even when no other human would."

Lisa and David

Lisa was just seventeen when a girlfriend asked David to drive her home. "I wasn't attracted to him at all. I thought he was weird. He was so quiet, he didn't say two words the whole time we were in the car." At the time David was dating someone else and so was she. They remained friends for a couple of years, and eventually started dating.

Not long after their wedding, Lisa realized that David liked pornography. "It wasn't like he tried to hide it, really. I'd catch him with the stuff, or I'd catch him pleasuring himself. I knew right away." She wasn't a bit happy about his habit. "I tried to tell him that the Bible said he shouldn't look with lust upon a woman. He looked at me like I was a space alien. He had no idea what I was talking about."

As a new Christian, Lisa attended church and read the Bible. "I knew that his porn was stealing from me. He went for long periods without any interest in sex—sometimes as long as six months." Her frustration led to angry outbursts and even threats. But David didn't stop.

David couldn't stop.

Instead, he tried harder to hide his obsession. As David rose in his business, he was asked to travel. Sometimes, his assignments lasted for three months, sometimes six. He traveled to China, to Portland, to San Francisco. After many years, Lisa began to believe that David was cheating on her. She became obsessed with knowing the truth. She searched the house and his shop. The truth came to light one day when she caught him communicating on-line with his mistress. Lisa was devastated.

He promised to change. They went to counseling. But David never expressed any genuine sorrow for the things he had done to hurt Lisa. In fact, he didn't seem to be sorry at all. Then, without making any real progress, he left for another assignment. "His new job was only a few hours from our home and during the whole time he was away, he never once came home. Not once."

Lisa knew something was very wrong.

She believed that David's behavior had escalated. She began to pray, asking God what to do. She sent him love notes, baking cookies and mailing them to him. And she prayed for David, not like she had before, but with a new fervancy. She prayed that his sin would drive him to real repentance. She asked God to make him miserable until his heart demanded that he come clean.

It worked. The next time David came home, Lisa asked him to attend a meeting with a counselor specializing in pornography. To her surprise, David agreed. There, his heart was changed.

David confessed his sin. His pornography addiction combined with long absences from home had allowed him to frequent prostitutes and to engage in multiple relationships with other women. Even now, Lisa does not know the full extent of his infidelity. She already has enough to forgive.

David's confession was followed by genuine repentance. He began counseling and joined a men's group. David met with a personal mentor. He entered into his recovery with the same enthusiasm that he had applied to his addiction. He read books. He completed workbooks. He joined support groups. His new life began about four years ago.

Today, David is a changed man. He prays with his wife every night before bed. He reads his Bible. He is fully present in their relationship for the first time in 36 years.

Lisa has had a difficult road. Forgiveness has cost more than she ever expected. In the process, she has struggled through significant depression. She lost her sense of humor and stopped caring for herself. People she once loved grew tired of the journey that filled her every waking thought.

Some friends fell away. Others wanted the old funny Lisa back. She struggled to stay centered. "I had a few friends who went through this with me. I wasn't completely alone. But it was hard. I quit doing all the things that I loved. I pulled back into this dark hole." Today Lisa has a counselor and attends a support group of her own. She has begun to regain her balance.

And Lisa has become a lioness. She hates pornography. "Pornography is a tool of the enemy. It has only one goal, to destroy the lives of the men who are caught in its trap. It will destroy those men, it will take down their marriages and it will obliterate their families. I hate it. I hate it."

Though the journey is one she wouldn't repeat, Lisa would marry David again. In fact, she did. Only July 11, 2012, the day after their 36th wedding anniversary, Lisa and David renewed their vows in front of their children, grandchildren and a few very close friends. The ceremony was full of gratitude and deep joy. The video captures the complete and deep love these two share. It also captures the cost of their reconciliation.

Today, Lisa loves David more than ever. "Why wouldn't I want to keep this amazing man?" But the cost for that man has been high—much higher than she'd ever imagined. Lisa understands that forgiveness is a process, a difficult, painful process.

She remains in the process. She shares her story here with one simple hope: Lisa hopes that other women will listen to her story and gather the courage to confront pornography in their home. She hopes that women will choose to do what she did not. She hopes they will take the example of Matthew 18 and make a quiet, reasoned appeal to their husbands. Then, if their husband will not listen, she hopes women will follow up by bringing other men (men who understand pornography) into the conversation. Then, if they are forced, women must escalate their battle. "Scripture is clear. We are to have absolutely nothing to do with this sin. We have to be willing to do battle for our men and for our families. We can't let fear keep us from the right course of action."

Lisa believes we must not let pornography take our nation.

Common Threads

As you read these stories, you may wonder, "What do these tales have to do with purity?" The answer? Everything.

It is purity which is destroyed by infidelity and pornography. It is purity which drives couples suffering from violence and illness to solve their issues and seek healing. It is purity which finds the strength to forgive. The strength to move forward. The strength to love again.

Purity. Exclusivity. One life-long vow.

These stories have other common threads. Did you notice that **in nearly every story, the couple involved seeks outside support?** They don't try to solve their problems on their own. Some find that support in groups. Others had counselors. One had a few close friends. This is a biblical truth. We are not to travail alone. We are to share our journey with other believers. Even Jesus took along a support group when he faced his biggest challenge. Peter and John accompanied him to the Garden of Gethsemane.

In each of these stories, one partner had the courage to initiate change. When one partner is bound by sin—whether pornography or infidelity or violence—they need someone to have courage for them. They need someone to have faith that change is possible. If the bound person could change themselves, if they could set themselves free, they would have. But they could not.

Notice too that in many of these stories a time of separation was necessary in order for the reluctant partner to seek healing. I have often observed that the church is terrified of marital separation. However, in many cases, that time away provides just enough pressure to pursuade the reluctant partner to seek help. By itself, separation is neither good nor bad. However, with the right help and structure, it can change the course of the marriage.

In most of these stories, one partner, through no fault of her own, is deeply wronged. Who knows exactly why a man gives in to sexual addiction or pornography or alcohol? But when these addictions take over a person's life, they take over a marriage. **When the healing begins, often one spouse discovers wrongs they had no idea existed. For the wronged spouse, forgiveness is neither instantaneous nor painless.**

Forgiveness takes work. It takes determination. It takes repetition. Some spouses refuse to begin that journey. Others begin and cannot finish. These women committed to the course. They were determined not to let the past control their future. When they were absolutely certain that the behavior had ended, that repentance was real, that recovery was genuine, they determined to let go of the past. It hasn't been easy.

One last thing. In all of these stories, someone took the first step. Sometimes, that step looks like a loving act, writing notes, giving gifts, inviting to events. Other times, that first step looks less loving. Confronting sin. Catching a spouse in a betrayal.

But love always wants the best thing for the one loved. Love wants her spouse to be free from pornography. Love wants her spouse to experience genuine intimacy. Love wants her spouse to know self control. In these stories love sometimes took the hard road, the painful way, in order to see that her spouse became all that God had in mind.

It would be much easier to let go, to divorce, to give up.

Taking the first step involves humility. It involves understanding our own sin, our own vulnerability. Taking the first step involves commitment, risk, and potential disappointment or rejection. It is always much easier to wait. To blame. To accuse. To let anger grow. To justify our bad attitude, our bitterness. After all he's done, we have every right to give up and walk away.

But these ladiies had the courage to choose a different way. A more difficult way. And the reward—a new husband, a **better** husband—cost them dearly. In the process, they got so much more. They were themselves changed. They experienced a new relationship and dependance on God. They experienced deeper relationships in the Body of Christ. The grew in understanding of themselves, and of the human soul.

They grew in compassion. In some cases, they discovered an entirely new ministry. Though it wasn't easy, they chose the deeper way. What about you? When impurity threatens to sweep away your home, what course will you choose?

Wrapping Up

Congratulations on making it through a long and difficult study. I hope that along the way you've learned a little bit about yourself and your spouse. I hope that you've begun to consider new ideas and concepts. I hope that you and your husband have experienced more delight in your intimate time together. Most of all, I hope that you've begun to think of your marriage journey in a new way.

Because your marriage is a journey.

Of course, your marriage is more than just your sexual relationship. It has many pillars, involving your finances, your parenting, your spiritual life, your direction, your calling. While your sexual relationship is very important, it is not your marriage. All the parts make up the whole, and all the parts will grow.

Today, you are not what you will be. You and your husband will both change and mature. Your body will age. Your love will deepen. You will face many challenges together.

My deepest hope is that nothing you face will ever cause you to opt out of your together journey. As you've probably surmised, my marriage hasn't been all that I'd hoped. As a twenty-year-old bride, I had no idea that we would face a miscarriage, numerous surgeries, cancer threats, and yes, even a long separation. I didn't know that we would need counseling. I never suspected that I would consider divorce.

But God was faithful. I want to tell you the story:

We had been married almost 18 years when our world imploded. We entered counseling shell shocked and deeply saddened. At the suggestion of our Christian therapist, we separated. During that year, I began to believe that we would never experience healing. No matter how hard I prayed, I could not forgive the wrongs I'd experienced. I couldn't let go and start over. The wounds were so deep and bled so freely, I thought divorce was the only option. I needed, more than anything, to stop the pain. We did therapy. I did therapy. We went to counseling together. I made no progress.

Then, one day, as I was driving near our home, I remember hearing the Lord speak to me. "Watch this," He said.

At that moment, I saw a rock wall appear in the upper corner of my vision (though I continued to drive without difficulty). The wall was made of mud and rock, the kind you might find between fields in some remote farming area. I remember thinking to myself. *Oh, that looks like a wall in Ireland.*

As I drove along still watching this vision, the wall exploded. Rocks flew everywhere. The vision was so real that I ducked away from the debris, as if rocks had flown into my windsheild. In that instant, I knew that the Holy Spirit had destroyed the resentment that had become a wall between my husband and myself. Gone.

I turned my car around and called my husband. "I think we need to talk," I told him. He begged off, giving me a list of things he needed to accomplish on his day off. "I'm not sure how long this is going to last," I said. "We should talk now."

Wrapping it Up

God's miraculous and instantaneous work was the first step in our reconciliation. In the twenty years since then, we've continued to build on that healing. It wasn't always easy. There have been frustrations, tears, misunderstandings. There have been set backs. But there has also been change.

Neither of us is the same as we were on our wedding day, so many years ago. God has loved us too much to leave us like that.

God loves you too. He wants to heal you when you cannot heal yourself. He wants to give you courage, strength and determination to follow Him when everyone around says, "give up." Though you may not experience a "vision," I can assure you, God's work in your heart is no less miraculous.

Your sexuality is a pillar in your relationship together. Just as crucial to that relationship as your finances or your parenting, your sexual relationship deserves your protection. It deserves to be cherished and developed. God designed it to protect your connection, to draw you together, to build your family.

He cares about how you use this divine gift. He wants to help you make it all it was meant to be.

I care about your marriage journey. Let me know how God uses this study. Contact me via my website and share your story: www.bettenordberg.com.

May God richly bless you as you follow Him!
Bette

Acknowledgements

To be honest, the idea for Pure Sex, Great Sex came not from me, but from good friend Gloria Penwell, widow of well-known editor Dan Penwell (AMG Publishers). In the spring of 2012, Gloria watched online as I responded to the 50 Shades controversy, and suggested I do a Bible study on the subject. Her proposed title, *50 Shades of Purity*, never made it to print. But the idea stuck with me. Thanks for the suggestion, Gloria!

I started writing in the summer of 2012, teaching the first study group that fall. I was re-writing by Christmas. In 2013, I assembled my own production team – an outstanding group of professionals, who happen to be people I love and respect. So many have contributed to the completion of this project. Kerry Latin and Cheryl Oliver read and supported the first classroom version. Jeannie St. John Taylor provided an excellent substantive edit for the second edition and Laura Davis provided line-editing. Good friend Susan Duplissey assisted with galley edits. Cover and page design were created by the talented Dallas Drotz of Drotz Design. Dallas has been a great help all along the way! Don Ottis, of Veritas Communication, contributed wisdom and marketing expertise. Good friends Naomi Hunt and Janet Boyer contributed wisdom and direction to the text.

Wrapping it Up

I owe much thanks to the many women I interviewed for this project. Among them therapist Connie McDonald, MS who provided her expertise in treatment of pornography addiction. Because of privacy, I cannot list all the names here; you know who you are. My deepest thanks for your bravery!

Titus tells us the older women should teach the younger women how to love their husbands. For the first time in my teaching career I am fulfilling that Biblical command to the letter! I have truly become an "older" woman. Over the years, I have had the privilege of so many deep and loving relationships; so many wise women have invested into my life. I think of Gwen Ellis, Marj Stuart, Linda Hickling, Elva Nordberg, Noni Faris, Naomi Hunt, Cheryl Oliver and so many, many more. God has been good to give me so many wise women-friends. I hope this project shares their wisdom with others.

Like listening to an older, wiser friend, I hope that you feel inspired and encouraged to make your marriage all it can be, with God's divine help!